TASTE
recipes for
entertaining

WILLIAMS-SONOMA

TASTE
recipes for entertaining

WELDON OWEN

During the past two years, many readers of *Williams-Sonoma TASTE* magazine have written to let us know that they appreciate the genuine enthusiasm for good food that they find in every issue. They recognize that our goal is to introduce the finest ingredients available, often even traveling to their place of origin, and to showcase both innovative and classic ideas on how to prepare them with style. Simply put, everything we do, we do in the spirit of honest good taste.

Our readers have also let us know that they like to welcome family and friends to their dinner tables, so we have compiled this, the second volume of *The Best of Taste,* with entertaining in mind. Any occasion, from a traditional holiday to a company party, is made more memorable with good food, beautifully prepared and served. To help make the planning go more smoothly, in addition to the usual chapters by course, we have assembled a chapter of seasonal menus, including a bountiful Sicilian Easter feast with roasted lamb as the centerpiece and an old-fashioned American Thanksgiving dinner with turkey and all the trimmings.

Of course, many other wonderful recipes can be found in these pages, too, from festive drinks to luscious desserts, eclectic appetizers to globe-hopping main courses, all of them easily slipped into a menu—and all of them guaranteed to make every get-together a celebration to remember.

— chuck williams

Throughout its second year of publication, *Williams-Sonoma TASTE* magazine continued to pack its pages with stories of some of the world's finest ingredients and most talented food artisans. Whenever our writers and photographers roamed around America and Europe in search of interesting dining and travel tales, they always returned with exciting accounts of delicious and often unusual dishes cooked by everyone from internationally celebrated chefs to enterprising street-food vendors. I have been lucky enough to join in some of these travels. We sampled creamy jasmine-scented ice cream in Palermo, Sicily, freshly boiled stone crab claws eaten right on the dock in Naples, Florida, a perfectly roasted Thanksgiving turkey in Walnut Creek, California, and herb-and-nettle-filled ravioli at a farm on Lummi Island, Washington. Many of these singular dishes have made their way into this second collection, *Taste Recipes for Entertaining*.

In searching for these sometimes elusive, always rewarding culinary experiences, everyone at the magazine has the same goal in mind: to create stories that encourage you to prepare the accompanying recipes whenever entertaining is on your calendar. I hope that the seasonal recipes and menu ideas that follow prove as inspirational and enjoyable to you as they have to all of us this past year at *Williams-Sonoma TASTE*.

— andy harris, editor-in-chief

1

Cocktails have come back into fashion. No matter what the celebration, there's a drink, or an assortment of drinks, to match or even set the tone of the party. Choosing what to serve is a matter of both style and taste: shaken or stirred, a classic rendition or an original creation, a generous dose of spirits or no spirits at all.

Sometimes you may want to serve a drink that recalls a favorite place, such as the efferverscent Bellini created at the legendary Harry's Bar in Venice. Other times the drink menu may be defined by the season. In winter, you can warm your guests with a selection of hot libations from around Europe, including spice-laced Scandinavian Glögg, the familiar British Hot Toddy, and the not-so-familiar French Apple Toddy, made with Calvados in place of whiskey. To cool off on a hot afternoon, consider the Mint Julep, an icon of the American South that demands the best locally produced bourbon. Or you might temper the heat of a summer day with tall glasses of Sangrita—the Mexican orange juice–based aperitif customarily partnered with a shot glass of tequila—or with a spirits-free, satisfyingly healthful Mango-Banana Smoothie from the Bahamas.

One thing many of these drinks have in common is their reliance on a simple sugar syrup, made by boiling together water and sugar. Mix up a good-size container of the syrup and store it in the refrigerator, and you'll always be ready for a party. Also, plan a drinks menu that doesn't keep you tied to the bar, rather than mingling with your guests. For a small gathering, individually mixed drinks are fine, but if you have invited a houseful of friends, plan to serve a bountiful punch or one or more blender drinks that can be turned out in big batches. Select your glassware with care, too, choosing shapes and sizes, from graceful hand-blown martini glasses to stocky tumblers, that will show off your drinks in style.

Sangrita

1¼ cups (10 fl oz/310 ml) fresh
orange juice

3½ tablespoons grenadine

pinch of red chile powder, preferably
pequín or cayenne

salt

½ cup (4 fl oz/125 ml) tequila

SERVES 2

Fruity and spicy, Sangritas (shown opposite along with shots of tequila) are a favorite Mexican drink, customarily served with shots of tequila alongside, to cool off a hot summer's day.

1 In a pitcher, combine orange juice, grenadine, and chile powder. Add salt to taste and stir. Refrigerate until cold.

2 Serve sangrita in 2 tall glasses, with tequila served alongside in 2 small glasses.

Campari Grapefruit Frappé

¼ cup (2 oz/60 g) sugar

1-inch (2.5-cm) piece fresh ginger,
peeled and thinly sliced

½ cup (4 fl oz/125 ml) Campari

2 cups (16 fl oz/500 ml) ruby red
grapefruit juice

1 lime, thinly sliced

SERVES 4

Campari is a popular Italian brand of bitters, a mixture of alcohol, spices, and herbs. Here, it's mixed with ruby red grapefruit juice, along with an invigorating punch of homemade fresh ginger syrup.

1 In a small saucepan, bring ¼ cup (2 fl oz/60 ml) water to a simmer over low heat. Add sugar and ginger and stir until sugar is dissolved. Remove from heat and let steep until syrup is room temperature. Discard ginger.

2 In a shaker, combine Campari, grapefruit juice, and lime slices. Add ginger syrup to taste and crushed ice. Shake and pour immediately into individual glasses.

Negroni

3 tablespoons (1½ fl oz/45 ml) gin

3 tablespoons (1½ fl oz/45 ml) sweet
vermouth

3 tablespoons (1½ fl oz/45 ml)
Campari

orange slice or twist

SERVES 1

Americans are masters of the cocktail, but Italians have some classics, too. Take the Negroni—the potent drink that mixes gin and sweet vermouth with Campari, a combination that's credited to Count Camillo Negroni, a 1920s cocktail-loving Florentine aristocrat. At Harry's Bar, they make a perfect Negroni and this is their recipe.

1 Pour gin, vermouth, and Campari into a glass half-filled with ice cubes. Stir briefly to mix. Add orange slice or twist. Or, in an ice-filled shaker, combine gin, vermouth, and Campari. Shake and strain into a chilled glass. Add orange slice or twist.

Glögg

½ cup (4 oz/125 g) sugar

1 bottle (12 fl oz/375 ml) brandy

8 whole cloves

½ cup (3 oz/90 g) raisins

½ cup (2½ oz/75 g) slivered blanched almonds

1 cup (8 fl oz/250 ml) ruby port

SERVES 6

This Scandinavian party punch is served hot and sweetened with a sugar, or simple, syrup. The syrup will keep indefinitely in the refrigerator and is useful for sweetening many kinds of punch as well as iced tea and cocktails.

1 In a large, nonaluminum saucepan with a lid, bring ½ cup (4 fl oz/125 ml) water to a simmer, uncovered, over medium-high heat. Add sugar and stir constantly until it completely dissolves.

2 Reduce heat to low, add brandy, cloves, raisins, and almonds, and stir to combine. Cook, uncovered, over low heat until warm.

3 Averting your face, carefully ignite brandy mixture with a match. Allow it to flame for about 20 seconds. Add port and stir with a wooden spoon until flames subside. If flames do not subside, cover saucepan with lid to extinguish.

4 Pour mixture into a serving pitcher and then ladle into small glasses.

Mango-Banana Smoothie

4 bananas

1 mango

SERVES 4

There are hundreds of versions of mango smoothies; perhaps the most restorative one is the sweet drink made by Nettie Symonette. Thickened with frozen bananas, it's perfect on a hot morning or afternoon at her eco-tourism resort, Nettie's Different of Abaco, in the northern archipelago of the Bahamas.

1 Peel bananas and cut crosswise into slices ¼ inch (6 mm) thick. Put in a bowl or plastic zip-lock bag, cover or seal, and freeze until hard.

2 To prepare mango, using a sharp knife set just off center to avoid the pit, slice mango lengthwise to remove 1 side. Repeat with other side. Place each half cut side up on a cutting board and score flesh in crosshatch pattern, cutting down to, but not through, skin. Press against skin with your thumbs, forcing mango cubes upward. Cut across bottom of cubes, freeing them from skin.

3 In a blender, purée mango with 2 tablespoons water. Add frozen bananas and purée until well blended.

Dune Cocktail

CREAM OF COCONUT

1 can (14 fl oz/430 ml) unsweetened coconut milk

⅓ cup sugar

2 tablespoons (1 fl oz/30 ml) gin

1 tablespoon (½ fl oz/15 ml) cointreau

splash blue curaçao

SERVES 1

This pale turquoise drink matches the color of the water outside chef Jean George Vongerichten's Ocean Club on Paradise Island in the Bahamas. It's made with cream of coconut, a sweet mixture that's not the same as coconut cream. You can find it in many supermarkets, or make it yourself (see recipe).

1 FOR CREAM OF COCONUT: In a saucepan, simmer unsweetened coconut milk with sugar, stirring, until sugar is dissolved. Let cool.

2 In a shaker with ice, combine gin, cointreau, curaçao, and 6 tablespoons (3 fl oz/90 ml) cream of coconut. Strain into a cocktail glass and serve.

The Perfect Mint Julep

40 small, fresh spearmint leaves, plus
sprigs for garnish

6 tablespoons (3 fl oz/90 ml) bourbon
whiskey, preferably Maker's Mark,
plus 3 cups (24 fl oz/750 ml)

1 cup (8 fl oz/250 ml) distilled water

1 cup (8 oz/250 g) granulated sugar

shaved ice

confectioners' (icing) sugar,
for dusting

SERVES 12–15

This Southern cocktail is required drinking at the Kentucky Derby and any parties associated with it. A debate rages: Should the mint be bruised or not? In Bill Samuels Jr.'s rendition, the drink is infused with bruised mint leaves, then served with whole ones.

1 Put mint leaves in a small bowl with 6 tablespoons of bourbon. Let soak for 15 minutes. Using a cheesecloth (muslin), gather up mint and wring bundle over bowl. Dip bundle in liquid and wring again. Repeat dipping and wringing process several times. Discard bundle. Set mint extract aside.

2 In a small saucepan, bring distilled water to a simmer over medium-high heat. Add granulated sugar and stir constantly until it completely dissolves. Let syrup cool to room temperature.

3 In a pitcher, combine 3 cups bourbon and 1 cup (8 fl oz/250 ml) syrup. Add mint extract to julep mixture 1 tablespoon at a time, tasting as you go, until there is a soft mint aroma and flavor, using about 3 table-spoons total of mint extract. Cover julep mixture tightly with a lid or plastic wrap and refrigerate until flavors marry, about 24 hours.

4 To serve, fill glasses halfway with shaved ice. Insert a mint sprig in each glass and then pack in more ice to about 1 inch (2.5 cm) above rim. Insert a straw cut to reach 1 inch (2.5 cm) above rim. When frost forms on surface of glasses, pour julep mixture over ice and add a dusting of confectioners' sugar.

Bellini

SUGAR SYRUP (OPTIONAL)

½ cup (4 oz/125 g) sugar

2 ripe white peaches, peeled, pitted,
and chopped

1 bottle (24 fl oz/750 ml) dry
Prosecco, well chilled

SERVES 8

One of the world's great aperitifs, a simple
but sublime concoction of white peach purée
and Prosecco, an Italian sparkling wine,
was created by the father of consummate host
Arrigo Cipriani for guests at his restaurant,
Harry's Bar, in Venice.

1 FOR OPTIONAL SUGAR SYRUP: In a small saucepan,
combine sugar and ½ cup (4 fl oz/125 ml) water
and stir until sugar is dissolved. Bring to a rolling boil
over high heat. Lower heat to a simmer and cook
until light syrup is formed, about 5 minutes. Remove
from heat and let cool.

2 Pass chopped peaches through a food mill placed
over a bowl. Pass coarse peach purée through a fine-
mesh sieve placed over a bowl, pressing with back
of a spoon. Taste and adjust sweetness, if needed,
with a little sugar syrup. Cover and refrigerate purée
until well chilled.

3 In a pitcher, combine peach purée and Prosecco.
Stir until well blended. Pour into well-chilled glasses.

Moscow Mule

3 tablespoons (1½ fl oz/45 ml) vodka

juice of ½ lime

¾–1 cup (6–8 fl oz/180–250 ml)
ginger beer or ginger ale

lime slice

SERVES 1

Invented in the 1940s in Hollywood, this drink gets its name from a mixture of Russian vodka and punchy ginger beer, which has the kick of a mule. Donata Maggipinto adds a squeeze of lime juice to hers, making it a frisky take on a vodka tonic.

1 Pour vodka and lime juice into a highball glass half-filled with ice cubes. Fill with ginger beer or ginger ale, stir, and add lime slice.

Fevergrass Tea

5 stalks lemongrass, cut in half
crosswise

SERVES 4

If you like, sweeten this refreshing beverage with a little honey or raw sugar.

1 In a saucepan, bring 8 cups (64 fl oz/2 l) water to a boil over high heat. Add lemongrass bottoms, lower heat to a simmer, and cook for 15 minutes. Remove from heat and let steep for 1 hour. Strain, discarding lemongrass bottoms.

2 Pour into ice-filled glasses and garnish with remaining halves of lemongrass.

Hot Buttered Rum

1 teaspoon sugar

3 whole cloves

¼ cup (2 fl oz/60 ml) dark rum

whole nutmeg, for grating

1 teaspoon unsalted butter

½ cinnamon stick

SERVES 1

Dark rum's rich and spicy flavor suits this time-honored recipe. Some versions call for the butter to float on top, but it's best stirred right into the warm rum. Like all good hot drinks, this is easily made in large quantities for a crowd.

1 Combine sugar, cloves, and rum in a tumbler or mug. Add ½ cup (4 fl oz/125 ml) boiling water.

2 Grate nutmeg to taste over top. Add butter and stir briefly with cinnamon stick. Serve immediately.

CONCOURS RÉGIONAL
DE POIRÉ

1999

MEDAILLE D'ARGENT

PASSAIS LA CONCEPTION

Hot Toddy

¼ cup (2 fl oz/60 ml) Scotch whisky

3 or 4 whole cloves

zest of 1 lemon, cut in a long
spiral strip

1 teaspoon honey

2 tablespoons fresh lemon juice

SERVES 1

This British classic was originally served cold,
until sailors decided to heat it up to keep warm.
It's the perfect restorative drink following an
afternoon of wintertime activities.

1 In a glass, combine whisky, cloves, and lemon zest.

2 Add honey, lemon juice, and ½ cup (4 fl oz/125 ml)
boiling water. Stir well. Serve immediately.

Apple Toddy

¼ cup (2 fl oz/60 ml) Calvados or
applejack

¼ cup (2 fl oz/60 ml) apple syrup

4 or 5 thin apple slices

whole nutmeg, for grating

SERVES 1

The French take on the Hot Toddy uses
Calvados or applejack, along with apple syrup,
giving the drink a sweeter scent and flavor
than the English original. When buying apple
syrup, look for the Austrian brand D'Arbo;
this company produces some of the best, most
intense fruit syrups on the market.

1 In a glass, combine Calvados or applejack and
apple syrup. Add ¼–½ cup (2–4 fl oz/60–125 ml)
boiling water and stir.

2 Add apple slices and grate nutmeg to taste over
top. Serve immediately.

2

Just as a good first impression contributes to a fruitful business meeting, a delectable appetizer paves the way to a successful party. Whether it's perfectly seared foie gras on a gold-rimmed plate accompanied with the requisite Champagne, or a passed hand-painted platter of crisp fried bites served with a rustic red wine, the starter establishes the style for what is to come. Hosts who want to depart from tradition can even assemble a buffet table of complementary appetizers and present them as the meal itself.

STARTERS

The first rule to selecting the ideal starter is to choose a dish that fits the occasion. If you're hosting a formal dinner, plump grilled scallops bathed in lemon juice and olive oil are a classic choice. For a more relaxed gathering, make a batch of Supplì al Telefono, a Roman favorite that calls for combining leftover risotto with mozzarella and basil, shaping the mixture into balls, and then deep-frying them. When a guest bites into one of these crisp, golden croquettes, long, thin strings of cheese are revealed—strands that recall the "telephone lines" for which the dish is named.

Some of the best appetizers can be served any time of year. For example, Asian-inspired Jumbo Roasted Shrimp, flavored with sesame oil, rice vinegar, and tamari, deliver a sunny taste that's equally welcome at a sit-down wintertime supper in front of the fireplace or at a summertime cocktail

party on the patio. Good-quality oysters are readily available at fish markets year-round, making them a perfect choice to launch nearly any party. Serve them on the half shell with an assortment of dipping sauces, such as a horseradish-spiked tomato sauce and a creamy mustard-dill sauce. To reduce your time in the kitchen, ask the fishmonger to shuck the oysters for you.

If more than one appetizer is being served, select recipes that are both complementary and are ready or nearly ready to serve as soon as the guests arrive. For example, pair a hot appetizer that can be assembled in advance and popped into the oven just as the party begins, with a cold appetizer that can be put out the moment the first guests walk through the door. Be sure to choose handsome serving platters, too, to make that good first impression.

Roasted Jumbo Shrimp

24 jumbo shrimp (prawns) in the
shell, about 2¾ lb (1.4 kg)
total weight

3 tablespoons Asian sesame oil

2 tablespoons rice wine vinegar

2 teaspoons tamari sauce

freshly ground black pepper

24 cilantro sprigs (fresh coriander)

SERVES 8

These shrimp become tender and succulent
when roasted at high heat. The simple Asian
flavors used here contrast deliciously with
the sweet shrimp, but you may also wish to try
other oil-and-vinegar combinations. Serve as
a first course or pass on an hors d'oeuvres tray.

1 Remove legs from shrimp, leaving shell and tail
intact. Lay each shrimp on its side and butterfly
by making a horizontal cut three-fourths of way
through curved side, from head end to just before
tail. Remove dark vein and discard.

2 Preheat oven to 500°F (260°C).

3 In a small bowl, combine sesame oil, vinegar,
tamari, and pepper to taste. Rub shrimp with oil mixture. In an 18-by-13-inch (45-by-33-cm) roasting or
broiling pan, arrange shrimp splayed out in butterflied
position, shell side up. Roast for 2½ minutes.

4 Turn shrimp. Drizzle with remaining oil mixture
and roast for 2½ minutes longer.

5 Divide shrimp among 8 serving plates, placing
shrimp flesh side up with tails in center of plate.
Garnish with cilantro sprigs.

Catalan Mixed Seafood Grill with Romesco Sauce

ROMESCO SAUCE

2 dried ají amarillo chiles

6 dried Hungarian cherry chiles

3 large tomatoes, cored (about 1½ lb/750 g)

½ cup (4 fl oz/125 ml) olive oil

2 slices whole-grain bread, crusts removed

1 small dried red chile

½ jalapeño chile, seeded and thinly sliced

4 cloves garlic, minced

¼ cup (1½ oz/45 g) each blanched almonds and blanched hazelnuts, lightly toasted

2 tablespoons finely chopped fresh flat-leaf (Italian) parsley

1 teaspoon smoked paprika

1 tablespoon red wine vinegar

2 teaspoons kosher salt, or to taste

½ lb (250 g) small squid, cleaned

½ lb (250 g) shrimp (prawns), shelled and deveined

½ lb (250 g) monkfish, cut into 1-inch (2.5-cm) cubes

¼ cup (2 fl oz/60 ml) olive oil

salt and freshly ground black pepper

18 each Manila or other small clams and mussels, scrubbed

SERVES 6

Ají amarillos are vibrant orange-colored Peruvian chiles available frozen or pickled in specialty-food stores. Dried anchos or nyoras can be substituted.

1 FOR ROMESCO SAUCE: Soak dried ají amarillo and Hungarian cherry chiles separately in warm water until softened, about 20 minutes. Using a small, sharp knife, remove stems and seeds and discard. Set chiles aside.

2 Preheat oven to 350°F (180°C). Cut tomatoes in half crosswise and gently squeeze out seeds. Lightly coat skins with olive oil and place cut side down on a lightly oiled baking sheet. Roast until skins are loosened, about 10 minutes. Let cool, remove skins, and chop coarsely.

3 In a skillet, heat 2 tablespoons of oil over medium heat. Add bread slices and cook, turning once, until lightly browned on both sides, about 4 minutes total. Drain on paper towels until cool enough to handle. Tear into large pieces. Set aside.

4 Heat another tablespoon of oil and sauté soaked chiles, dried red chile, and jalapeño chile over medium heat until just fragrant, about 1 minute.

5 In a food processor, combine bread, chiles, garlic, nuts, and parsley and process until a thick paste forms. Add tomatoes, paprika, vinegar, salt, and remaining olive oil and process until incorporated. Taste and adjust seasoning with more salt, if desired. Transfer to a bowl and set aside.

6 Preheat grill on medium-high heat. In a bowl, combine squid, shrimp, and monkfish. Add olive oil, salt, and pepper and toss to coat fish. Grill until cooked through, 2–3 minutes.

7 Discard any clams or mussels that do not close when touched. Grill clams and mussels until shells open, 1–2 minutes.

8 Arrange on a serving platter and serve with romesco sauce.

Crisp-Fried
Baby Artichokes

OLIVE PASTE

4 oz (125 g) gaeta olives, pitted

2 cloves garlic

2 large anchovy fillets
in oil, drained

1 tablespoon capers

pinch of dried thyme

pinch of cayenne pepper

2 tablespoons extra-virgin
olive oil

1 tablespoon fresh lemon juice

12 baby artichokes

salt and freshly ground
black pepper

vegetable oil, for deep-frying

SERVES 4

Flattening the cleaned baby artichokes before frying, a classic technique, gives these appetizers an attractive, flowerlike presentation. Serve the olive tapenade in a bowl on the side or drizzled around the plate.

1 FOR OLIVE PASTE: In a food processor, combine and roughly chop olives, garlic, anchovies, capers, thyme, and cayenne. Then, while machine is running, pour olive oil in a steady stream into mixture. Finely chop but do not completely purée. Transfer to a bowl, adjust seasoning if needed, and add lemon juice. Cover and set aside.

2 Trim stem of each artichoke, leaving about 1 inch (2.5 cm) intact. Gently ease each artichoke open. Scoop out fuzzy choke, if any, and discard. Invert artichokes and place on a cutting board. Flatten and spread out leaves by pushing down on base of each. Season to taste with salt and pepper.

3 In a deep pan, pour in about 1½ inches (4 cm) oil and heat over high heat. When oil reaches 250°F (120°C) on a deep-frying thermometer, add inverted artichokes to pan and gently cook, turning frequently, until base of each artichoke is tender when pierced with a sharp knife, 5–8 minutes. Carefully regulate heat to prevent oil from becoming too hot and frying artichokes too quickly. Transfer to paper towels to drain.

4 Transfer artichokes, still inverted, to cutting board and gently press on each base so leaves spread more. Raise oil heat to 350°F (180°C). Have ready a cup of cold water. Return inverted artichokes to oil and cook for 1–2 minutes, then turn them over. Standing at arm's length, sprinkle with a little water to make them extra crisp. Drain and serve hot or warm with olive paste.

Crisp Breaded Tomato Slices with Mozzarella and Marjoram

4 or 5 slices white or whole-wheat (wholemeal) bread, crusts removed

sea salt and freshly ground black pepper

1 cup (5 oz/155 g) all-purpose (plain) flour

1 egg, beaten

1 teaspoon milk or heavy (double) cream

3 tomatoes, cored and cut into 12 slices ½ inch (12 mm) thick

unsalted butter or olive oil, for frying

¼ lb (125 g) fresh mozzarella cheese, drained and cut into 12 slices ⅛ inch (3 mm) thick

1 scant tablespoon chopped fresh marjoram

SERVES 2–4

Crisp on the outside, but warm and juicy inside, Deborah Madison's fried tomatoes can be served as a delicious side dish or a delightful lunch with green salad.

1 In a food processor, process bread into fine crumbs. You should have about 1½ cups (3 oz/90 g). Season to taste with salt and pepper.

2 Spread flour on a large plate. Combine egg with milk or cream and pour onto a second plate, and spread seasoned bread crumbs on a third plate. Coat tomato slices first in flour, then egg, and finally bread crumbs.

3 In a large nonstick skillet, heat 2–3 tablespoons butter or olive oil over medium heat. When hot, add tomatoes and cook, covered, until browned on the bottom, 3–5 minutes. Uncover pan and turn over tomatoes, adding more butter or oil if needed, to brown other side. Lay a slice of mozzarella on each tomato and recover pan. Cook until bread crumbs are browned and cheese is melted, 3–5 minutes. Remove from heat and transfer to a platter.

4 Garnish with chopped marjoram and serve immediately.

Spicy Marinated Artichokes

FLAVORED OIL

2 cups (16 fl oz/500 ml) extra-virgin
olive oil

4 fresh thyme sprigs

3 cloves garlic, unpeeled
and smashed

3 strips lemon zest

½ teaspoon red pepper flakes

1 teaspoon whole black
peppercorns

9 baby artichokes

juice of 1 lemon

salt and freshly ground
black pepper

1 carrot, peeled and cut into sticks

1 onion, cut into wedges

¼ cup (2 fl oz/60 ml) extra-virgin
olive oil

1 cup (8 fl oz/250 ml) dry white wine

MAKES TWO ½-PINT (8–FL OZ/250-ML) JARS

These spice-infused baby artichokes are great to keep on hand for impromptu entertaining since they will last for a few weeks in the refrigerator. Serve them on toasted bread with goat cheese that has been marinated in a separate jar of this spicy oil.

1 FOR FLAVORED OIL: In a small saucepan over low heat, combine all 6 ingredients. Gently warm until mixture is just heated; do not allow to bubble. Remove from heat and let cool uncovered.

2 Meanwhile, prepare artichokes. Fill a large bowl with cold water and lemon juice. Pull off outermost layer of tough leaves from artichokes. Peel and trim stems, removing ⅛ inch (3 mm) from each base. Halve each artichoke lengthwise and gently scoop out fuzzy choke if prickly to the touch. As each artichoke is prepared, submerge in lemon water to prevent discoloring.

3 Drain artichokes and pat dry on paper towels. Season to taste with salt and pepper. Put carrot and onion in a large sauté pan and arrange artichokes in a single layer on top. Drizzle with olive oil and wine. Cook over high heat until mixture starts to bubble, then lower heat to a simmer. Cover and cook until artichoke bases and leaves are tender, about 35 minutes. Remove from heat, let cool completely in a pan, and then discard braising vegetables and juices. Divide artichokes evenly between 2 sterilized ½-pint (8–fl oz/250-ml) jars. Pour in cold flavored oil. Tightly seal jars and store in a cool, dark place for 3 days. Once jars are opened, store in refrigerator.

Artichokes Barigoule

4 large artichokes, stems removed

½ oz (15 g) dried morel mushrooms, soaked in 1 cup (8 fl oz/250 ml) hot water for 1 hour

3 oz (90 g) bacon, finely diced

2 tablespoons unsalted butter

2-oz (60-g) piece Bayonne or Serrano ham, finely diced

1 tablespoon finely chopped fresh chives

1 tablespoon finely chopped fresh flat-leaf (Italian) parsley

freshly ground black pepper

4 tablespoons (2 fl oz/60 ml) extra-virgin olive oil

1 large carrot, peeled and cut into sticks

1 large onion, cut into wedges

1 clove garlic, finely chopped

2 fresh savory sprigs or 1 teaspoon dried

1 cup (8 fl oz/250 ml) dry white wine

4 slices sourdough or rye bread, toasted, rubbed with cut halves of 1 clove garlic, and brushed with melted butter

SERVES 4

For this version of the Provençal favorite, large slices of toasted sourdough or rye bread are brushed with melted butter and garlic. Make sure that the artichoke bottoms are flat so they sit securely on the toasts.

1 Pull off outermost layer of tough leaves and cut 1 inch (2.5 cm) off top of each artichoke. Then snip off thorny tips of leaves. Gently ease each artichoke open. Scoop out fuzzy choke and discard. Set aside.

2 Drain morels, reserving liquid. Pat dry on paper towels, then finely chop. In a sauté pan over high heat, cook bacon in its fat until crisp, about 5 minutes. Add morels and 1 tablespoon butter. Continue to sauté until morels soak up pan juices, 2–3 minutes. Transfer to a bowl and stir in ham, chives, and parsley. Season to taste with pepper.

3 Ease prepared artichokes open. Spoon in morel mixture, filling to top of each artichoke; do not overfill.

4 Pour 2 tablespoons oil into a large pot. Add carrot and onion, then sprinkle in garlic and savory. Strain reserved morel liquid and pour into pot with enough water to just cover vegetables. Place artichokes upright in 1 layer and pour in wine and remaining oil. Cover artichokes loosely with parchment (baking) paper. Bring liquid to a boil over high heat, then lower heat to achieve a simmer and cover pan. Cook until base of each artichoke feels soft when gently pierced with tip of a knife and leaves detach easily when pulled, about 1½ hours.

5 Remove artichokes and keep warm. Remove all braising ingredients from cooking juices and discard; return juices to heat. If not syrupy, reduce over high heat until you have about ¾ cup (6 fl oz/180 ml), 2–3 minutes. Lower heat and stir in remaining butter. Divide sauce among 4 shallow bowls and serve each artichoke on top of a slice of garlic toast.

Kashmiri Lamb Meatballs

4 tablespoons canola oil

1 onion, finely chopped

¾ lb (375 g) lean ground (minced) lamb

1 egg, lightly beaten

½ cup (1 oz/30 g) fresh bread crumbs

2 teaspoons finely chopped garlic

1 teaspoon ground coriander

½ teaspoon chile powder

1 teaspoon salt

⅓ cup (½ oz/15 g) chopped fresh cilantro
(fresh coriander)

9 dried apricots, quartered

SERVES 10

Traditionally, these tender meatballs are cooked and eaten in a curry sauce with cashews, but they make wonderful appetizers served on their own. Try dipping them in yogurt flavored with lemon and chopped cilantro, or accompanying them with a store-bought chutney or spicy Indian pickle.

1 In a large skillet , heat 2 tablespoons canola oil over medium-low heat. Add onion and sauté until soft, about 6 minutes. Transfer onion to a bowl. Wipe out pan with a paper towel and set aside.

2 Add remaining ingredients, except apricots and remaining oil, to bowl with sautéed onion. Mix well, using your hands.

3 Scoop up a rounded teaspoonful of the mixture. Insert 1 dried apricot quarter in middle, forming meat mixture around it to make a ball. Repeat with remaining meat mixture and apricot quarters.

4 Heat 1 tablespoon of remaining oil over medium heat in same skillet. Add half of meatballs and sauté, gently shaking pan, until browned on all sides, 8–10 minutes. Using a slotted spoon, transfer to paper towels to drain briefly. Repeat with remaining 1 tablespoon oil and meatballs.

Salmon and Potato Kebabs with Peruvian Chiles

1 tablespoon ají amarillo purée

2 tablespoons olive oil

1 lb (500 g) skinless salmon fillet,
cut into eighteen 1½-inch
(4-cm) cubes

12 waxy fingerling potatoes, peeled

6 ají amarillo chiles packed in brine,
halved and seeded

SERVES 6

This recipe calls for two kinds of ají amarillo, the vibrant orange-colored Peruvian chile. They're available whole, packed in brine, or as a purée. Look for them in specialty-food stores. If you can't find them, omit the purée and use another kind of pickled chile, such as pepperoncini.

1 Preheat grill on high heat.

2 If using wooden skewers, soak 6 wooden skewers in water for 30 minutes. Set aside.

3 Mix ají amarillo purée and 1 tablespoon olive oil. Add salmon cubes and marinate, covered, in refrigerator for 30 minutes.

4 In a saucepan, cover potatoes with salted water and bring to a boil over high heat. Reduce heat to achieve a simmer and cook until just tender, 12–15 minutes. Drain and let cool.

5 With a thin skewer, gently pre-pierce potatoes. In a bowl, toss potatoes and whole ají amarillo chiles with remaining 1 tablespoon olive oil.

6 Skewer a piece of salmon, chile, and potato and repeat, ending with salmon.

7 Grill each kebab, turning once until salmon is cooked through, about 4 minutes on each side.

Ricotta-Filled Zucchini Blossoms

12 large zucchini blossoms, stems intact if desired

1¼ cups (10 oz/315 g) whole-milk ricotta cheese

1 egg, lightly beaten

¾ cup (3 oz/90 g) freshly grated Parmigiano-Reggiano cheese

2 tablespoons chopped fresh flat-leaf (Italian) parsley

fine sea salt and freshly ground black pepper

1 clove garlic, finely chopped

2 tablespoons extra-virgin olive oil

2 lb (1 kg) ripe tomatoes, peeled, seeded, and chopped (optional)

1 teaspoon sugar (optional)

SERVES 6

There is one cardinal rule for zucchini blossoms: Treat them gently. At the Wine and Culinary Center of the centuries-old Tuscan estate Capezzana, cooking students are taught to stuff the flowers carefully with a garlic-spiked ricotta mixture and then cook them quickly in hot oil or tomato sauce, so the blossoms don't get soggy.

1 Gently rinse zucchini blossoms. Transfer to paper towels and pat dry.

2 In a bowl, combine ricotta, egg, Parmigiano-Reggiano, and parsley. Season generously with sea salt and pepper. Stir until well blended.

3 Transfer cheese mixture to a pastry bag fitted with plain tip or a plastic bag with ½ inch (12 mm) cut off corner. Pipe mixture into zucchini blossoms.

4 In a large nonstick skillet, drizzle garlic with olive oil. Cook over medium heat until garlic is sizzling. If serving in tomato sauce, add tomatoes and cook for 5 minutes longer. Season to taste with sea salt and pepper. Taste and add sugar if needed.

5 Add zucchini blossoms to garlic oil or tomato sauce and cook until heated through, about 5 minutes. Serve immediately.

Supplì al Telefono

3 cups (24 fl oz/750 ml) vegetable or chicken stock

2 tablespoons olive oil

1 clove garlic, crushed

1 cup (7 oz/220 g) Carnaroli rice

¼ cup (2 fl oz/60 ml) dry white wine

½ cup (2½ oz/75 g) drained, oil-packed, sun-dried tomatoes, cut into strips

salt and freshly ground black pepper

½ cup (4 fl oz/250 ml) heavy (double) cream

2 tablespoons butter

½ cup (2 oz/60 ml) grated Parmesan cheese

¾ cup (1 oz/30 g) basil leaves, torn into small bits

¼ lb (125 g) fresh mozzarella, drained and finely diced into ¼-inch (6-mm) cubes

½ cup (2½ oz/75 g) all-purpose (plain) flour

2 eggs, beaten

1½–2 cups (6–8 oz/185–250 g) fine dried white bread crumbs

vegetable oil, for deep-frying

MAKES 24

Risotto balls can be made with Carnaroli, Arborio, or any other member of the starchy, short-grain rice family. This enchanting dish is named for the telephone line–like strands of cheese that form when the balls are bitten into.

1 In a saucepan, bring stock to a gentle simmer.

2 In a heavy-bottomed risotto pan or sauté pan, heat olive oil over medium-low heat and gently sauté garlic until just soft. Stir in rice and cook for 2 minutes until rice is coated with oil, is partially transparent, and begins to make a clicking noise. Quickly add wine and stir constantly until liquid is absorbed.

3 Add stock a ladleful at a time, stirring constantly until liquid is absorbed before next addition. When half of stock has been added, stir in sun-dried tomatoes and season to taste with salt and pepper. Continue adding stock in the same manner, followed by cream, until rice is al dente.

4 Remove from heat and stir in butter, Parmesan, and basil. Cover pan and let rest for 3 minutes. Uncover pan and stir, adjusting seasoning if needed. Spread risotto in a shallow dish and let cool completely.

5 Shape 1 tablespoon of cold risotto into a walnut-sized ball molded around 1 mozzarella cube. Repeat to make 24 balls.

6 Spread flour on a plate. Pour eggs onto a second plate and spread bread crumbs on a third plate. Coat rice balls first in flour, then eggs, and finally bread crumbs.

7 In a deep skillet, pour in vegetable oil to a depth of 3 inches (7.5 cm) and heat to 350°F (180°C) on a deep-frying thermometer. Cook rice balls in batches of 4 until golden all over, 2–3 minutes. If cooked too quickly, cheese in middle will not melt. Drain on paper towels and keep warm in a low oven while cooking the remaining rice balls. Serve warm.

Platter of Oysters and Three Sauces

CHAMPAGNE-MIGNONETTE SAUCE

¾ cup (6 fl oz/180 ml) champagne vinegar

6 tablespoons (2 oz/60 g) minced shallots

¼ teaspoon kosher salt

¼ teaspoon freshly ground white pepper

HORSERADISH-TOMATO SAUCE

1 cup (8 oz/250 g) tomato ketchup

2 tablespoons prepared horseradish, or more to taste

2 teaspoons Tabasco or other hot-pepper sauce, or more to taste

1 tablespoon fresh lime juice

kosher salt and freshly ground black pepper

MUSTARD-DILL SAUCE

1 cup (8 fl oz/250 ml) mayonnaise

1 tablespoon Dijon mustard

3 tablespoons finely chopped fresh dill

2 teaspoons freshly grated lemon zest

kosher salt and freshly ground white pepper

1 or 2 bags crushed ice

36 oysters, shucked, shells and liquid reserved

lemon wedges, for garnish

SERVES 6

Buy your oysters from a reputable fishmonger. If possible, have the oysters shucked for you; be sure to take the shells and the oyster liquid as well. The beauty of serving oysters at a party is that they need no preparation, once the job of opening them is done. Serve shucked oysters on ice on the same day that you buy them.

1 FOR CHAMPAGNE-MIGNONETTE SAUCE: In a small bowl, combine vinegar and shallots. Add kosher salt and white pepper. Stir to blend well. Cover and refrigerate until ready to serve.

2 FOR HORSERADISH-TOMATO SAUCE: In a small bowl, combine ketchup, horseradish, Tabasco, and lime juice. Season to taste with kosher salt and pepper. Stir to blend well. Cover and refrigerate until ready to serve.

3 FOR MUSTARD-DILL SAUCE: In a small bowl, combine mayonnaise, mustard, dill, and lemon zest. Season to taste with kosher salt and pepper. Stir to blend well. Cover and refrigerate until ready to serve.

4 Make a bed of crushed ice on a large platter. Arrange oysters with their liquid in shell halves on ice. Serve accompanied with three sauces and lemon wedges.

Grilled Marinated Scallops with Lemon and Olive Oil

36 sea scallops, tough side muscle removed, rinsed, and patted dry

¼ cup (2 oz/60 ml) olive oil

zest of 1 lemon, cut into wide strips

DIPPING SAUCE

6 tablespoons (3 fl oz/90 ml) extra-virgin olive oil

juice of 1 lemon

sea salt and freshly ground black pepper

SERVES 6

Simplicity itself, sea scallops are briefly marinated then served with a Greek-style lemon and oil mixture. A grill's smoky flavor is part of the dish's appeal, but the skewers can also be broiled in a hot oven.

1 Preheat grill on high heat or prepare a fire in a charcoal grill. Soak 12 wooden skewers in water for 30 minutes.

2 In a bowl, combine scallops with oil and lemon zest strips. Cover and marinate in refrigerator for 30 minutes.

3 FOR DIPPING SAUCE: In a bowl, combine oil and lemon juice. Season to taste with salt and pepper.

4 Thread 3 scallops onto each skewer and season to taste with salt and pepper. Grill until scallops are just barely cooked through, about 2 minutes on each side. Serve immediately with dipping sauce.

3

Two of the most popular items on menus, soup and salad, have plenty in common. They can require a pantryful of exotic ingredients or no more than a trio of basics They can take hours of shopping and preparation, or they can be thrown together in minutes with what's on hand. They can play the role of a light, refreshing first course or of a hearty, filling main dish. And although soups are typically served hot and salads cold, they can also easily trade temperatures. In fact, soups and salads can be whatever you want them to be.

soups
& salads

The similarities don't stop there. Both soups and salads boast a repertory of classics, but they also both invite innovation. The time-honored Venetian Risi e Bisi, made with creamy Vialone Nano or Arborio rice and fresh peas, is always a hit, but so too is Barbara Kafka's thoroughly modern version of old-fashioned mushroom and barley soup, to which she adds a handful of fragrant, earthy porcini. Butter (Boston) lettuce tossed with a vinaigrette will never go out of style, but the wide variety of lettuces, from baby greens to potent microgreens (tiny but fully developed leaves), now offered at

many markets has transformed today's salad options. The practice of using the same ingredient in two forms turns up in salads as well as soups, as in Tamarind-Chile Duck and Tatsoi Salad, which features tatsoi at different stages of maturity, and Deborah Madison's lovely tomato and pepper soup topped with fried tomato skins.

A well-designed party menu is one that allows you to prepare some dishes in advance. Many soups can be made a day or more ahead of time and refrigerated or frozen, freeing you up to concentrate on dishes that need your undivided attention just before serving. Salads, of course, are usually assembled at the last minute, but you can often ready their components—wash and crisp the lettuce, whisk together the dressing, toast the croutons—hours before your guests begin to ring the doorbell.

Pea Pod Soup

2 lb (1 kg) fresh peas, in the pod

6 cups (48 fl oz/1.5 l) chicken stock

kosher salt and freshly ground
black pepper

2 egg yolks

½ cup (4 fl oz/125 ml) heavy (double)
cream, plus more
for garnish

SERVES 4

With an unusual twist, Barbara Kafka uses
the pods but not the peas for her delicious and
uncomplicated first-course soup. The rules,
however, remain the same: Use the freshest pea
pods you can find.

1 Shell peas by pulling the strings. Discard tips
and strings of pods. Reserve peas for another use.
Wash and rinse pods.

2 In a large saucepan over high heat, bring stock to
a boil. Season to taste with kosher salt and pepper.
Add pods, stir well, and lower heat to achieve a
simmer. Cook, partially covered, until pods are very
tender, about 45 minutes.

3 In 2 or 3 batches, purée pods and stock in food
processor. Strain through a fine-mesh sieve, firmly
pushing on solids. Discard solids. Return purée to
saucepan and reheat over medium heat.

4 In a small bowl, beat egg yolks lightly with ½ cup
(4 fl oz/125 ml) cream. Stirring constantly, pour a
small amount of hot soup into egg-cream mixture
to temper it. Stir mixture back into soup. Cook over
medium heat, stirring constantly, until soup thickens
slightly and coats back of spoon. Serve garnished
with cream swirled into each bowl.

Tomato and Roasted Pepper Soup with Fried Tomato Skins

1½ lb (750 g) ripe tomatoes, cored and bottoms scored

3 red bell peppers (capsicums), grilled or roasted, skins removed

3 tablespoons olive oil

1 onion, finely diced

pinch of saffron threads

1 bay leaf

leaves plucked from 2 fresh thyme sprigs

1 teaspoon sweet paprika or ½ teaspoon smoked Spanish paprika

2 cloves garlic, finely chopped with a pinch of salt to form a paste, plus 1 small clove garlic

1 tablespoon tomato paste

sea salt and freshly ground black pepper

4 cups (32 fl oz/1 l) vegetable stock, chicken stock, or water

3 tablespoons chopped fresh flat-leaf (Italian) parsley

SERVES 6

Tomato skins are often discarded when cooking; in this recipe from Deborah Madison, they're ingenuously fried for a tasty garnish. Grilling the bell peppers lends a lightly smoky flavor to the late summer dish.

1 In a large saucepan of boiling water, dip tomatoes for 10–15 seconds, then remove. Peel tomatoes and reserve skins for garnish. Halve tomatoes crosswise. Using a sieve to catch seeds, squeeze juice into a bowl and set aside. Discard seeds. Scoop out pulp from inner walls of tomatoes and finely dice. Cut remaining outer portions of tomatoes into ¼-inch (6-mm) dice.

2 Remove seeds and veins from roasted bell peppers and cut into ¼-inch (6-mm) dice.

3 In a large pot, warm 2 tablespoons olive oil and add onion, bell peppers, saffron, bay leaf, thyme leaves, and paprika. Cook over medium heat, stirring occasionally, until onion begins to soften, about 6 minutes. Add chopped garlic paste, tomato paste, and 1 teaspoon sea salt. Stir well, add ¼ cup (2 fl oz/60 ml) water, and cook for 5 minutes. Add tomatoes, reserved tomato juice, and stock, and bring to a boil. Lower heat to low and simmer, partially covered, for 20–25 minutes. Season to taste with sea salt and pepper.

4 Finely chop parsley together with remaining clove garlic and a pinch of sea salt. Set aside.

5 Just before serving, in a small nonstick skillet, heat remaining 1 tablespoon olive oil over medium-high heat. When hot, add reserved tomato skins in a single layer and fry in batches, turning constantly until crispy, about 2 minutes. Remove from heat and sprinkle with sea salt. Garnish soup with chopped parsley mixture and fried tomato skins.

Mushroom-Barley Soup

½ oz (15 g) dried porcini mushrooms

1 cup (7 oz/220 g) pearl barley

2 teaspoons kosher salt, plus
salt to taste

1 carrot, peeled and finely diced

2 small stalks celery, strings
removed, finely diced

1 tablespoon unsalted butter

1 onion, finely chopped

¼ lb (4 oz/125 g) white mushrooms,
thinly sliced

3 cloves garlic, finely chopped

1 tablespoon chopped celery leaves

¼ cup (⅓ oz/10 g) chopped fresh dill

freshly ground black pepper

SERVES 8

Barbara Kafka uses reconstituted dried porcini mushrooms to add depth of flavor to her restorative soup. If you're not inclined to strain the soaking liquid, let it settle for several minutes instead, and then slowly pour it into a bowl, stopping before you reach the sediment.

1 In a small saucepan, bring 1 cup (8 fl oz/250 ml) water to a boil. Add porcini and simmer briskly for 2 minutes. Remove porcini with slotted spoon and press with another spoon, letting liquid drip back into saucepan. Chop porcini coarsely and set aside. Strain liquid through a sieve lined with dampened cheesecloth (muslin) or a coffee filter. Set aside.

2 In a pot, bring 8 cups (64 fl oz/2 l) water to a boil. Add barley, 2 teaspoons kosher salt, carrot, celery, and porcini. Lower heat to low, cover, and simmer for 30 minutes.

3 Meanwhile, in a sauté pan over medium heat, melt butter. Add onion and cook, stirring occasionally, until soft, 5 minutes. Add fresh mushrooms and cook until they begin to brown and turn slightly glossy, 5 minutes more. Transfer mixture to a bowl.

4 In same sauté pan over medium heat, pour in mushroom soaking liquid and bring to a boil, stirring and scraping pan with a wooden spoon. Transfer mushroom liquid and mushroom mixture to barley mixture in pot. Bring to a boil, then lower heat and simmer, covered, for 10 minutes. Stir in garlic and simmer, covered, for 5 minutes longer.

5 Remove from heat and stir in celery leaves and dill. Season to taste with kosher salt and pepper.

Risi e Bisi

½ lb (250 g) green (spring) onions, including a few pale green tops, cut into 2-inch (5-cm) pieces

2 cups (3 oz/90 g) packed spinach leaves

2 tablespoons packed fresh flat-leaf (Italian) parsley leaves

¼ cup (2 fl oz/60 ml) olive oil

1 cup (7 oz/220 g) Vialone Nano rice

5–6 cups (40–48 fl oz/1.25–1.5 l) chicken stock

1½ cups (7½ oz/235 g) shelled English peas (about 1 lb/500 g in the shell) or frozen peas

kosher salt and freshly ground black pepper

fresh Parmesan cheese shavings, for garnish

SERVES 4

For this Venetian spring dish, use enough stock so that the rice-and-pea mixture remains soupy. Vialone Nano is a tiny, almost transparent short-grain Italian rice; you can also use Arborio.

1 In a food processor, finely chop (but do not purée) green onions, spinach, and parsley.

2 In a large saucepan over high heat, heat olive oil. Add rice and sauté for 2 minutes. Lower heat to medium. Add stock, a ladleful at a time, stirring frequently, until about half of stock has been added and absorbed, about 15 minutes. Stir in peas and chopped green onion, spinach, and parsley mixture. Continue adding stock and cook until peas are tender, about 5 minutes. Consistency should be soupy; add more stock if needed. Season to taste with salt and pepper. Garnish with Parmesan cheese shavings.

Tomato and Tuna Salad with Zucchini

1 lb (500 g) fresh ahi tuna

½ cup (4 oz/125 g) capers, rinsed and drained

3 fresh bay leaves

2–3 cups (16–24 fl oz/500–750 ml) extra-virgin olive oil

4 small zucchini (courgettes), cut into 1-inch (2.5-cm) pieces

½ lb (250 g) cherry tomatoes, halved and seeded

salt and freshly ground white pepper

2 tablespoons finely chopped fresh flat-leaf (Italian) parsley

SERVES 4

Italians like to cook tuna by simmering it, then marinating it in olive oil—and Arrigo Cipriani is no exception. He tosses the flaky fish with fresh vegetables and capers for a satisfying salad that's ideal for luncheon alfresco.

1 Bring a large pot of salted water to a boil over high heat. Add tuna and lower heat to a simmer. Poach until just cooked, 10–12 minutes.

2 Transfer tuna to a cutting board, pat dry, and let cool. Cut tuna into 6 pieces and place in a shallow dish. Sprinkle with capers and bay leaves. Pour in enough olive oil to cover tuna. Cover dish and refrigerate for 24 hours.

3 Bring a saucepan of salted water to a boil over high heat. Add zucchini and cook until crisp-tender, 2–3 minutes. Immediately transfer to a bowl of cold water to halt cooking. Drain and set aside.

4 Remove tuna from oil, transfer to a bowl, and flake into bite-sized pieces. Using a slotted spoon, transfer capers to bowl of tuna. Discard bay leaves and oil. Add zucchini and tomatoes to tuna and toss gently. Season to taste with salt and white pepper and sprinkle with parsley.

Wild Rice Salad
with Chestnuts

1 cup (6 oz/185 g) wild rice

½ teaspoon salt, plus more to taste

2 large radishes, thinly sliced

2 green onions, including tender
green tops, thinly sliced

¼ lb (125 g) peeled roasted
chestnuts, sliced

freshly ground black pepper

4½ teaspoons cider vinegar

¼ teaspoon prepared mustard

6 tablespoons plus 1½ teaspoons
vegetable oil

SERVES 4–6

An exciting mix of nutty flavors and a variety
of textures from chewy wild rice to crumbly
chestnuts and crisp radishes make Fran Gage's
salad an interesting dish to include at a
dinner party.

1 Rinse rice in cold water, then drain. In a large
saucepan, combine rice, ½ teaspoon salt, and 4 cups
(32 fl oz/1 l) cold water. Bring to a simmer over
low heat, cover, and cook until rice is al dente, about
40 minutes. Drain rice in a large sieve. Rinse with
cold water and set aside to let cool. Rice may be
prepared a few days ahead.

2 In a large bowl, combine cooked rice, radishes,
green onions, and chestnuts. Season to taste with
salt and pepper.

3 In a small bowl, whisk together vinegar and
mustard. Slowly whisk in oil. Pour dressing over rice
salad and mix well.

Tamarind-Chile Duck and Tatsoi Salad

2 boneless duck breasts (1½ lb/750 g total weight), trimmed

1 teaspoon fine sea salt

½ teaspoon five-spice powder

1 tablespoon tamarind pulp

2 tablespoons fresh lime juice

2 tablespoons fish sauce

1 tablespoon dark brown sugar

1 or 2 red chiles, sliced

1 tablespoon sunflower oil

12 oz (375 g) tatsoi, each sprig halved

6 oz (185 g) baby tatsoi

lime slices, for garnish

SERVES 4

This seared duck salad features the delicate mustardy flavor of Chinese tatsoi prepared two ways: Large leaves are wilted in the exotically accented hot dressing and then tossed with bite-sized baby tatsoi.

1 Make 4 diagonal slits in skin of each duck breast. Rub all over with salt and five-spice powder. In a large sauté pan over low heat, cook duck, fat side down, until fat starts to melt, about 5 minutes. Raise heat to medium and fry, 5–8 minutes. Turn duck and cook until meat is just slightly pink inside, about 5 minutes longer. Transfer duck to a cutting board and let stand for 10 minutes.

2 Meanwhile, in a small bowl, combine tamarind pulp, lime juice, fish sauce, brown sugar, chiles, and sunflower oil.

3 Wipe out sauté pan, set over low heat, and slowly heat dressing mixture until bubbling. Add tatsoi sprigs, turn to coat with dressing, and cook until just wilted, about 1 minute. Transfer to large bowl, add baby tatsoi, and toss. Thinly slice duck and toss with tatsoi mixture. Garnish with lime slices.

Chicken Liver and Dandelion Salad

The unbeatable combination of chicken livers and bacon is the basis for this substantial salad, with dandelion greens adding a pleasant bite. Toasted buttered baguette slices are a required accompaniment.

BAGUETTE TOASTS

½ thin baguette

4 tablespoons (2 oz/60 g) unsalted butter, melted

salt and freshly ground black pepper

8 oz (250 g) medium-large dandelion leaves

½ lb (250 g) chicken livers

salt and freshly ground black pepper

1 tablespoon all-purpose (plain) flour

5 tablespoons (2½ fl oz/75 ml) olive oil

¼ lb (125 g) bacon, cut into thin strips

2 shallots, finely chopped

3 tablespoons red wine vinegar

¼ teaspoon Dijon mustard

pinch of sugar

2 tablespoons sunflower oil

1 oz (30 g) baby dandelion leaves

SERVES 4

1 FOR BAGUETTE TOASTS: Preheat oven to 350°F (180°C). Cut baguette into diagonal slices ⅛ inch (3 mm) thick. Brush both sides of slices with melted butter and season to taste with salt and pepper. Toast in oven for 10 minutes. Set aside.

2 Tear medium-large dandelion leaves in half and put in a large bowl.

3 Clean and trim chicken livers and cut in half. Season to taste with salt and pepper. Sprinkle with flour.

4 In a sauté pan over medium-high heat, heat 2 tablespoons olive oil. Add bacon and cook, stirring, until crisp, 5–8 minutes. Transfer bacon to paper towels to drain. Add shallots to fat in pan, lower heat to medium-low, and cook until soft, 3–5 minutes. Leaving juices in pan, transfer shallots to bowl of torn dandelion leaves. Add bacon on top.

5 Add 1 tablespoon olive oil to fat in pan and heat over medium-high heat. Add chicken livers and sauté, turning often, until browned outside but still pink inside, 3–5 minutes. Transfer livers to a cutting board.

6 Add vinegar to pan and cook until juices are bubbling, 1–2 minutes. Lower heat to low and stir in mustard, sugar, sunflower oil, and remaining 2 tablespoons olive oil. Season to taste with salt and pepper. Pour mixture over torn dandelion leaves, shallots, and bacon and toss.

7 Divide tossed salad among 4 plates. Top each portion with 2 toasted baguette slices. Cut livers in half once again. Top salads with livers and baby dandelion leaves. Serve immediately.

Baby Artichoke Salad with Truffles

8 cups (64 fl oz/2 l) vegetable stock

4 fresh thyme sprigs, plus
1 tablespoon fresh thyme leaves,
finely chopped

1 lemon, halved, plus juice of 1 lemon

12 baby artichokes

1 shallot, finely chopped

2 tablespoons sherry vinegar

¼ cup (2 fl oz/60 ml) grapeseed oil

¼ cup (2 fl oz/60 ml) extra-virgin
olive oil

1 oz (30 g) black truffle, finely
chopped, or a few drops of truffle oil

salt and freshly ground black pepper

1 head frisée lettuce, leaves separated

3 cups (3 oz/90 g) baby spinach,
stemmed

SERVES 4

Matt Millea, chef at Cielo restaurant at Big Sur's Ventana Inn, loves earthy truffles. Slivered truffles are sprinkled on his baby artichoke salad, making it a voluptuous first course.

1 In a large saucepan, combine vegetable stock with thyme sprigs and lemon halves. Bring to a simmer over medium heat.

2 Meanwhile, trim outer leaves and stems of baby artichokes, and cut tops ½ inch (12 mm) above hearts. Add artichokes to simmering stock and cook until just tender, about 20 minutes. Drain and let cool.

3 In a small bowl, combine the shallot, chopped thyme, vinegar, and lemon juice. Whisk in grapeseed oil and olive oil. Whisk in chopped truffle or truffle oil to taste.

4 In another bowl, toss cooked artichokes with half of vinaigrette. Season to taste with salt and pepper. Arrange 3 artichokes in a ring on 4 salad plates. Toss frisée and spinach in bowl with remaining vinaigrette. Season to taste with salt and pepper. Mound greens in center of each ring of artichokes.

Preparing a meal that reflects the season, its mood, and its produce might seem challenging but is, in fact, much easier than you would think. Here we have assembled four seasonal menus to show you how. From a spring feast with the Ravida family in Sicily to a Californian summer lunch with Donata Maggipinto, from a homey Thanksgiving dinner with Marion Cunningham to a Christmas eve in New York City with Mario Batali, the world of taste awaits.

seasonal
menus

spring menu

UOVA ALLA MONACALE

119

PASTA AND SARDINE TIMBALE

120

ROASTED EASTER LAMB WITH
WILD GREENS

123

CHOCOLATE-ALMOND TORTA

124

Uova alla Monacale

12 slices day-old white bread,
crusts removed

PARMESAN BÉCHAMEL SAUCE

1 tablespoon unsalted butter

2 tablespoons all-purpose (plain) flour

½ cup (4 fl oz/125 ml) milk

1 tablespoon freshly grated Parmesan

salt

6 hard-boiled eggs

1½ cups (7½ oz/235 g) all-purpose
(plain) flour

salt and freshly ground black pepper

1 egg, lightly beaten

1½ cups (12 fl oz/375 ml) olive oil, for frying

SERVES 6

These "friar's eggs" are part of the Ravida family's Sicilian *fritto misto,* or deep-fried snacks. The eggs are French in origin—note the addition of béchamel sauce—the cuisine of France having been popular with aristocratic Sicilians in the eighteenth century.

1 Preheat oven to 200°F (95°C). Lay bread flat on a large, ungreased baking sheet and toast in oven until dry, 25–30 minutes. Let cool, then break into pieces and add to a food processor. Process until fine crumbs are formed, 20–30 seconds. You should have about 1 cup (4 oz/125 g) bread crumbs. Set aside.

2 FOR PARMESAN BÉCHAMEL SAUCE: In a small saucepan, melt butter over low heat. Whisk in flour and cook for 1 minute. Remove from heat and gradually stir in milk, blending well. Return pan to medium heat and cook, stirring constantly, until very thick, about 5 minutes. Remove from heat and stir in Parmesan until melted. Season to taste with salt. Pour into a bowl and cover with plastic wrap pressed directly on surface. Let cool completely.

3 Cut hard-boiled eggs in half lengthwise and scoop out yolks. In a small bowl, mix yolks with 2 tablespoons béchamel. (Reserve remaining béchamel in the refrigerator for another use.) Spoon mixture back into egg cavities and firmly press down.

4 Spread flour on a large plate and season to taste with salt and pepper. Pour beaten egg onto a second plate and spread bread crumbs on a third plate. Coat each egg half first with flour, then beaten egg, and finally bread crumbs.

5 In a skillet, pour olive oil to a depth of 1 inch (2.5 cm) and heat to 350–375°F (180°–190°C) on a deep-frying thermometer. Fry egg halves in batches of 6, turning once, until golden, 2–3 minutes on each side. Drain on paper towels. Keep eggs warm in a low oven until all are cooked. Serve immediately.

Pasta and Sardine Timbale

1 lb (500 g) baby fennel, trimmed and
chopped into 1-inch (2.5-cm) lengths

salt

8 anchovy fillets

2 teaspoons extra-virgin
olive oil, plus more for oiling pan

¼ cup (2 fl oz/60 ml) olive oil,
plus 3 tablespoons

1 small onion, chopped

3 tablespoons dry white wine

1 clove garlic, chopped

2 pinches of saffron threads, soaked
in 2 tablespoons hot water

2 tablespoons tomato purée

¼ cup (1½ oz/45 g) pine nuts

¼ cup (1½ oz/45 g) raisins

3 tablespoons finely chopped
fresh flat-leaf (Italian) parsley

2 lb (1 kg) fresh sardines, scaled,
gutted, and filleted

1 lb (500 g) ziti pasta

1 cup (4 oz/125 g) dried bread
crumbs (see page 119)

freshly ground black pepper

SERVES 6

1 Preheat oven to 400°F (200°C). Bring a large pot of salted water to a boil. Add fennel, lower heat to a simmer, and cook until soft, about 30 minutes; reserve fennel cooking liquid. Put anchovies in a bowl and add 2 teaspoons extra-virgin olive oil. Set bowl over simmering water and mash until creamy.

2 In a large saucepan, heat ¼ cup olive oil over medium-high heat. Add onion and sauté for 3 minutes. Stir in wine, lower heat to low, and cook until onion just starts to turn golden, about 10 minutes. Add garlic and cook for 1 minute longer. Stir in saffron mixture, anchovies, tomato purée, pine nuts, and raisins. Add fennel and cook for 5 minutes longer, adding a little fennel cooking liquid if mixture looks dry.

3 Meanwhile, in a large skillet over low heat, combine 3 tablespoons water, 3 tablespoons olive oil, and chopped parsley. Add sardines, raise heat to medium, and cook, tossing carefully, until just cooked through, about 5 minutes.

4 Simultaneously, bring pot of fennel cooking liquid to a rolling boil, add pasta, and stir. Return to a boil, then lower heat to a gentle simmer and cook until al dente, about 12 minutes. Drain, reserving liquid. Add pasta to onion mixture, adding a little cooking liquid if mixture is too thick. Add one-fourth of sardines and gently toss.

5 Brush a 12-inch (30-cm) round baking pan with extra-virgin olive oil. Coat with bread crumbs, shaking pan to spread evenly. Tap to remove excess bread crumbs and reserve.

6 Set aside 4–6 sardines. Spread one-third of remaining sardines on bottom of pan, then season to taste with pepper. Spread half of pasta mixture in pan, then top with half of remaining sardines. Add remaining pasta, then sardines. Season to taste with pepper. Sprinkle with reserved bread crumbs.

7 Bake until golden brown, 25–35 minutes. Let cool slightly, then run a knife around inside edge of pan and invert onto a large serving plate. Garnish with reserved sardines.

Roasted Easter Lamb
with Wild Greens

4 lb (2 kg) young lamb, including
6 loin chops and 8 rib chops, cut into
3-inch (7.5-cm) chunks about 1 inch
(2.5 cm) thick, bones included

salt and freshly ground black pepper

⅓ cup (3 fl oz/80 ml) extra-virgin
olive oil

2 bay leaves

1 red onion, sliced into rings

GREENS
4 lb (2 kg) mixed wild greens

salt

2 tablespoons extra-virgin olive oil

freshly ground black pepper

fresh lemon juice or vinegar

SERVES 6

Because there are so few ingredients, the quality of each counts tremendously. Order young lamb, which is often available at Easter, from your butcher. Use the freshest wild greens available such as dandelion greens and nettles.

1 Preheat oven to 500°F (260°C).

2 Season lamb chunks to taste with salt and pepper. Put in a large roasting pan. Add olive oil, bay leaves, and onion. Toss to coat meat.

3 Roast uncovered for 30 minutes. Turn meat over, lower oven temperature to 350°F (180°C), cover pan with aluminum foil, and cook for 1 hour longer. Meat should be very tender, to point that it falls off bone.

4 Meanwhile, prepare greens: Trim greens and wash several times in cold water. Put greens in a large pot of salted water. Bring to a boil, keeping greens immersed. When water is at a rolling boil, lower heat to medium and simmer greens until very tender, 25–30 minutes.

5 Drain greens and transfer to a large serving dish. Drizzle with olive oil. Season to taste with pepper and add lemon juice or vinegar. Serve alongside lamb.

Chocolate-Almond Torta

1 cup (8 oz/250 g) plus 2 tablespoons butter, softened

1 cup (8 oz/250 g) plus 1 tablespoon
superfine (caster) sugar

1 teaspoon vanilla extract (essence)

5 eggs

7 oz (220 g) bittersweet chocolate,
finely chopped

11 oz (345 g) ground blanched
almonds

confectioners' (icing) sugar,
for dusting

SERVES 6–8

Nuts are a staple of many Italian pastries such as this moist and quite simple chocolate torta. Be careful when grinding the almonds not to turn them into a paste. If using a food processor, use the pulse button and grind them in batches.

1 Preheat oven to 325°F (165°C). Lightly grease a 10½-inch (26.5-cm) round cake pan that is at least 2 inches (5 cm) deep. Line bottom with buttered parchment (baking) paper. Set aside.

2 In bowl of a standing mixer fitted with paddle attachment, cream butter and superfine sugar until very light and fluffy. Add vanilla. Beat in eggs one at a time, beating well after each addition. Fold in chocolate and almonds.

3 Spread mixture in prepared pan. Bake until a wooden skewer inserted into center comes out clean, about 45 minutes.

4 Remove from oven and let cool in pan for 10 minutes. Run a knife around inside edge of pan and invert onto a wire rack. Carefully peel off parchment and let cool completely. Dust with confectioners' sugar.

summer menu

ZUCCHINI BASIL FRITATTITAS

129

SPICED CHICKPEAS

129

LAMB BURGERS WITH BLUE CHEESE AND
PARSLEY-MINT PESTO

130

COUSCOUS SALAD WITH FRESH CHERRIES

133

MINTED FAVA BEAN
AND CHERRY TOMATO SALAD

134

BLACKBERRY FOOL WITH FRUIT SALAD

137

Lamb Burgers with Blue Cheese and Parsley-Mint Pesto

6 oz (185 g) blue cheese,
at room temperature

3 lb (1.5 kg) ground (minced) lamb

3 tablespoons finely chopped fresh flat-leaf
(Italian) parsley

2 teaspoons finely chopped fresh rosemary

kosher salt and freshly ground
black pepper

PARSLEY-MINT PESTO

¾ cup (¾ oz/20 g) fresh flat-leaf
(Italian) parsley

¼ cup (¼ oz/7 g) fresh mint leaves

3 cloves garlic, coarsely chopped

¼ cup (2 fl oz/60 ml) extra-virgin olive oil

¼ cup (1 oz/30 g) freshly grated
Parmesan cheese

2 tablespoons pine nuts

½ teaspoon salt

6 pita breads

SERVES 6

For Donata Maggipinto, "casual" is the watchword when it comes to entertaining. Her menus are straightforward but delicious, like these blue cheese–stuffed lamb burgers. Serve them in pita breads, for a nice change from the standard buns.

1 Preheat grill on medium heat.

2 Divide cheese evenly into 6 pieces and shape each piece into a 2-inch (5-cm) disk. Set aside.

3 In a bowl, combine lamb, parsley, and rosemary. Season to taste with kosher salt and pepper. Mix gently; do not over-mix. Divide lamb into 6 portions. Shape each portion into a rough ball, molding it around a piece of cheese, then flatten slightly into a 4-inch (10-cm) round patty, making sure cheese is completely encased within. Put patties on a tray lined with plastic wrap, cover, and refrigerate until needed.

4 FOR PESTO: In a food processor, combine parsley, mint, garlic, and olive oil. Process until smooth. Add Parmesan, pine nuts, and salt. Process until well blended.

5 Grill patties, turning once, until cheese is melted and meat is medium-rare, 4–5 minutes on each side.

6 Split open pita breads and spread a dab of pesto inside. Fill each pita with a grilled patty and serve immediately.

Couscous Salad
with Fresh Cherries

2½ cups (20 fl oz/625 ml)
chicken stock

1½ cups (9 oz/280 g) couscous

salt

3 tablespoons extra-virgin olive oil

½ teaspoon chile oil, or more to taste

1½ teaspoons freshly grated
orange zest

2 tablespoons fresh orange juice

1 tablespoon fresh lemon juice

freshly ground black pepper

¼ cup (1 oz/30 g) pitted, diced fresh
cherries or dried cherries

3 green (spring) onions, cut into
1-inch (2.5-cm) lengths

4½ teaspoons finely chopped fresh
flat-leaf (Italian) parsley

SERVES 6

Deep red summertime cherries enliven this grain salad. If you want to serve it when cherries aren't abundant, or are prohibitively expensive, substitute dried cherries or other dried fruit.

1 In a saucepan, bring chicken stock to a boil. Put couscous in a large bowl and pour boiling stock over it. Add a generous pinch of salt and stir. Cover bowl with plastic wrap and let stand until couscous has absorbed stock and is tender, about 15 minutes.

2 Meanwhile, in a small bowl, combine olive oil, chile oil, and orange zest. Stir in orange juice and lemon juice. Season to taste with salt and pepper.

3 Using a fork, fluff couscous. Add cherries and green onions. Pour dressing over couscous and toss. Let stand at room temperature for at least 1 hour. Just before serving, stir in parsley. Taste and adjust seasoning, if needed, with chile oil, salt, and pepper.

Minted Fava Bean and Cherry Tomato Salad

4½ teaspoons fresh lemon juice

salt and freshly ground black pepper

3 tablespoons extra-virgin olive oil

3 cups (21 oz/655 g) fresh or frozen
fava beans

1 cup (6 oz/185 g) cherry
tomatoes, halved

4 green (spring) onions,
finely chopped

¼ cup (¼ oz/7 g) fresh mint leaves

SERVES 6

This salad has just the right ratio of crunchiness
to juicy flavor, and it's the perfect accompaniment
to Lamb Burgers with Blue Cheese and Parsley-
Mint Pesto (page 130). You can't beat the nuttiness
of fresh fava beans, but, if necessary, you can
substitute baby limas.

1 In a large bowl, whisk together lemon juice and salt
and pepper to taste. Add olive oil in a slow, steady
stream, whisking constantly. Set aside.

2 In a saucepan, bring water to a boil and add a generous pinch of salt. When water returns to a boil,
add fava beans and cook until tender, about 1 minute.
Drain. If using fresh fava beans, let cool until they can
be handled, then, with tip of a knife, slit skin of each
bean along side and pinch to remove bean. Discard skin.

3 Add fava beans, cherry tomatoes, green onions, and
mint to bowl of dressing and toss. Season to taste
with salt and pepper.

autumn menu

---⠿---

ROAST STUFFED TURKEY WITH
PAN GRAVY

141

FRESH SAGE STUFFING

144

CRANBERRY SAUCE

144

MASHED BAKED SQUASH WITH
MAPLE SYRUP

145

BAKING POWDER BISCUITS

148

PUMPKIN PIE

151

Roast Stuffed Turkey with Pan Gravy

1 fresh 12-lb (6-kg) turkey, at room temperature

1 recipe Fresh Sage Stuffing (page 144)

½ cup (4 oz/125 g) butter, softened

salt and freshly ground black pepper

GRAVY

butter, if needed

6 tablespoons (2 oz/60 g) all-purpose (plain) flour

salt and freshly ground black pepper

4 cups (32 fl oz/1 l) turkey or chicken stock

SERVES 6–8

1 Preheat oven to 325°F (165°C).

2 Remove giblets from turkey cavity and discard. Rinse turkey inside and out and pat dry with paper towels. Stuff body and neck cavities of turkey with sage stuffing. Tie legs together with kitchen string and secure loose skin with 2 turkey lacers. Fold wings underneath body. Rub butter over turkey, coating it thoroughly. Season to taste with salt and pepper. Line a roasting rack with greased parchment (baking) paper or grease rack well and place in a large roasting pan. Place turkey on rack, breast side down.

3 Roast turkey for 1 hour. Wearing clean oven mitts to protect your hands, turn turkey over breast side up. Return turkey to oven and roast until an instant-read thermometer registers 170°F (77°C) when inserted into breast and 185°F (85°C) when inserted into thigh, about 2 hours longer. Transfer turkey to a warm platter and cover loosely with aluminum foil. Let stand for at least 15 minutes.

4 Pour off all but ½ cup (4 fl oz/125 ml) pan drippings from roasting pan. If there is less than that, add melted butter to make up the difference.

5 Place roasting pan on stove top over medium heat and scrape bottom of pan to loosen all browned bits. Add flour and stir constantly until lightly browned, 3–4 minutes.

6 Season to taste with salt and pepper. Slowly pour in stock, stirring constantly. Cook, stirring, until gravy is smooth and thickened, about 2 minutes. Simmer for about 10 minutes longer to develop flavor. Serve immediately alongside turkey.

Pumpkin Pie

PIE DOUGH

1½ cups (7½ oz/235 g) all-purpose (plain) flour

¼ teaspoon salt

½ cup (4 oz/125 g) vegetable shortening

FILLING

2 cups (16 oz/500 g) pumpkin purée

3 eggs

1½ cups (12 fl oz/375 ml) heavy (double) cream

¾ cup (6 oz/185 g) firmly packed brown sugar

½ teaspoon salt

1½ teaspoons ground cinnamon

1 teaspoon ground ginger

½ teaspoon ground nutmeg

¼ teaspoon ground cloves

¼ teaspoon ground allspice

SERVES 8

Pumpkin pie is a classic component of the traditional Thanksgiving menu. Whipped cream or vanilla ice cream are requisite accompaniments, although the pie is delicious all by itself.

1 Preheat oven to 450°F (230°C).

2 FOR PIE DOUGH: In a bowl, combine flour and salt. Add shortening and, with a pastry blender, 2 knives, or your fingertips, work it into flour until mixture resembles coarse crumbs. Sprinkle 3–4 tablespoons (1½–2 fl oz/ 45–60 ml) ice water over flour mixture, a tablespoon at a time, stirring lightly with a fork after each addition; use just enough water so that dough holds together. Shape dough into a thick disk. Wrap in plastic wrap and refrigerate for 30 minutes.

3 On a lightly floured surface, roll out dough ⅛ inch (3 mm) thick. Transfer to a 9-inch (23-cm) pie pan. Trim edges to fit and crimp edges, if desired. Prick pie shell several times with a fork. Line shell with aluminum foil and fill with pie weights or dried beans. Bake for 6 minutes. Remove weights and foil. Continue baking until pie shell just begins to brown, about 4 minutes longer.

4 FOR FILLING: In a large bowl, beat together pumpkin purée and eggs. Add cream, brown sugar, salt, and spices. Beat until smooth.

5 Pour filling into pie shell and bake for 10 minutes. Lower oven temperature to 300°F (150°C) and continue baking until filling is nearly set, 30–40 minutes. (A sharp knife will come out almost clean, with traces of custard on it. Center of pie should not be completely firm.) Transfer to a wire rack and let cool.

―――――― ✺ ――――――

FRITTO MISTO AMALFI

155

CLAM AND MUSSEL SOUP

156

GRILLED SHRIMP IN LEMON LEAVES

159

WHOLE RED SNAPPER WITH
OLIVES AND CAPERS

162

ENDIVE SALAD WITH PARMESAN

165

SORRENTINE TORTA

166

Fritto Misto Amalfi

8 cups (64 fl oz/2 l) extra-virgin olive oil, for frying

½ lb (250 g) calamari, cleaned, bodies sliced into thin rings

½ lb (250 g) tiny smelts, cleaned

½ lb (250 g) fresh anchovies, cleaned

½ lb (250 g) small scallops, shucked and cleaned

2 lemons, thinly sliced

2 cups (8 oz/250 g) cornstarch (cornflour)

salt and freshly ground pepper

2 lemons cut into wedges, for garnish

SERVES 4

If fresh smelts and anchovies are not available, substitute any other fresh mixed seafood, as long as it is cut small enough to cook in a short time. Thinly sliced lemons are delicious as a fried accompaniment.

1 In a deep fryer, heat olive oil to 375°F (190°C) on a deep-frying thermometer. In a wide, shallow bowl, combine half the seafood and half the lemon slices. Sprinkle evenly with 1 cup (4 oz/125 g) cornstarch and, using your hands, toss quickly to coat.

2 Place coated mixture into a large sieve and tap it sharply to remove excess cornstarch. Add seafood and lemon mixture to hot oil and deep-fry until golden brown and crisp, about 1 minute. Remove from oil and transfer to a plate lined with paper towels. Season to taste with salt and pepper.

3 Immediately coat remaining seafood and lemon slices with cornstarch and repeat frying procedure. Transfer to a plate lined with paper towels. Season to taste with salt and pepper. Transfer to a serving dish. Serve immediately, accompanied with lemon wedges.

Clam and Mussel Soup

2 cups (16 fl oz/500 ml) white wine

3 lb (1.5 kg) mussels, scrubbed and debearded

2 lb (1 kg) clams, scrubbed

½ cup (4 fl oz/120 ml) extra-virgin olive oil

1 red onion, cut into ¼-inch (6-mm) dice

2 red bell peppers (capsicums), cut into ¼-inch (6-mm) dice

2 stalks celery, cut into ¼-inch (6-mm) dice

1 carrot, cut into ⅛-inch (3-mm) dice

3 salted anchovy fillets, rinsed and chopped

¼ cup (2 fl oz/60 ml) red wine vinegar, plus more if needed

2 cloves garlic, thinly sliced

8 slices country-style bread

¼ cup (⅓ oz/10 g) chopped fresh flat-leaf (Italian) parsley

SERVES 8

In Italy, it's traditional to enjoy a Christmas Eve dinner featuring various types of seafood. Mario Batali makes this colorful, shellfish-stocked soup as part of his classic Italian Christmas Eve menu.

1 Pour ½ cup (4 fl oz/125 ml) wine in each of 2 large pots. Discard any mussels or clams that do not close to the touch. Add mussels to one pot and clams to other. Cover both pots and bring liquid to a boil over high heat. Lower heat to a brisk simmer and cook until mussels and clams have opened, 2–4 minutes for mussels, 3–5 minutes for clams. Discard any shellfish that didn't open. Transfer shellfish to a bowl, reserving cooking liquid, and let cool. Shuck mussels and clams and discard shells. Strain reserved cooking liquid through a sieve lined with dampened cheesecloth (muslin) or a paper towel and set aside.

2 Preheat oven to 400°F (200°C).

3 In a large soup pot, heat ¼ cup (2 fl oz/60 ml) olive oil over medium-low heat. Add onion, bell peppers, celery, and carrot and sauté until vegetables are soft but not browned, 5–6 minutes. Add reserved shellfish-cooking liquid, remaining 1 cup wine (8 fl oz/250 ml), anchovies, vinegar, and garlic. Bring to a boil, then reduce heat and simmer until vegetables are tender, about 15 minutes. Add shellfish and heat without boiling. Taste and adjust seasoning, if needed, with more vinegar.

4 Meanwhile, toast bread slices in oven until golden brown, 6–7 minutes. Divide soup among 8 warmed bowls. Drizzle a little of remaining ¼ cup (2 fl oz/60 ml) olive oil over each serving. Sprinkle with parsley, float a slice of toast on top, and serve.

Grilled Shrimp in Lemon Leaves

1⅓ cups (11 fl oz/340 ml) extra-virgin olive oil

juice and grated zest of 3 lemons

1 teaspoon salt

2 tablespoons Sambuca or other anise liqueur

2 teaspoons whole fennel seeds, plus 1 teaspoon, crushed

12–18 large shrimp (prawns), peeled and deveined, tails intact

12–18 fresh lemon leaves

SERVES 6

Because lemons—and lemon leaves—are available year-round, these giant sweet shrimp can be served any time. Try to use organic lemon leaves; look for them at flower markets.

1 Preheat a grill or a broiler.

2 In a small saucepan, heat 1 cup (8 fl oz/250 ml) olive oil over medium-high heat to almost boiling. Remove from heat. Add juice and zest of 2 lemons, ½ teaspoon salt, Sambuca, and 2 teaspoons fennel seeds. Cover pan and let stand for 30 minutes.

3 Meanwhile, put shrimp in a large bowl. In a small bowl, combine remaining ⅓ cup (3 fl oz/90 ml) oil, lemon juice and zest, ½ teaspoon salt, and 1 teaspoon crushed fennel seeds. Whisk to blend well. Pour over shrimp and rub to coat well.

4 Return pan of scented oil to stove top and reheat gently over low heat until very warm but not hot.

5 Wrap each shrimp in a lemon leaf and secure with toothpicks. Grill or broil shrimp for 2 minutes on one side. Turn them over and grill 1 minute on other side. Serve immediately with warmed oil in a bowl for dipping. Provide a second bowl for discarded leaves and toothpicks.

Endive Salad
with Parmesan

2 tablespoons balsamic vinegar

salt and freshly ground black pepper

3 tablespoons olive oil

4 heads endive or Treviso radicchio,
trimmed and separated into leaves

2 oz (60 g) Parmesan cheese,
thinly shaved

SERVES 4

When guests unexpectedly drop by, this ultra-simple Italian-style salad is ideal: It's attractive and made with just a handful of ingredients that require minimal preparation.

1 Pour vinegar into a small bowl and season to taste with salt and pepper. Slowly whisk in olive oil until well blended.

2 In a large bowl, combine endive or radicchio leaves and Parmesan shavings. Drizzle with dressing and toss gently.

Sorrentine Torta

1½ cups (6 oz/185 g) walnut pieces

1 cup (4 oz/125 g) walnut halves

6 eggs, separated

1½ cups (6 oz/185 g) plus
1 tablespoon confectioners' (icing)
sugar, plus more for dusting

1 cup (5 oz/155 g) all-purpose
(plain) flour

½ cup (4 fl oz/120 ml) plus
1 tablespoon maraschino liqueur

2 cups (16 fl oz/500 ml) heavy
(double) cream

SERVES 8–10

1 Preheat oven to 400°F (200°C). Butter a 10-inch (25-cm) tart pan with a removable bottom.

2 Spread walnut pieces and walnut halves on separate baking sheets. Place both in oven and toast until nuts are fragrant and lightly golden, 5–10 minutes. Transfer walnut pieces to a cutting board, chop roughly, and set aside separately from walnut halves.

3 Using an electric mixer, in a large bowl, beat egg yolks and 1½ cups (6 oz/185 g) confectioners' sugar until mixture is thick and pale yellow and a slowly dissolving ribbon forms when a beater is drawn through mixture, about 5 minutes. Add flour and chopped walnuts and stir to combine.

4 In a separate bowl, with clean beaters, beat egg whites until stiff peaks form. Add one-third of egg whites to bowl with yolk mixture and stir well. Fold remaining whites gently but thoroughly into yolk mixture.

5 Pour batter into prepared tart pan. Bake until set and golden brown, about 30 minutes. Remove from oven and let cool on a wire rack for 30 minutes. Using a serrated knife, carefully cut cake in half horizontally. Place bottom half cut side up on a serving plate. Brush cut side with ¼ cup (2 fl oz/60 ml) maraschino liqueur.

6 In a large bowl, beat cream until soft peaks form. Add 1 tablespoon confectioners' sugar and 1 tablespoon maraschino liqueur and beat until stiff peaks form.

7 Spread bottom half of cake with half of whipped cream. Brush cut side of second cake half with remaining ¼ cup (2 fl oz/60 ml) maraschino liqueur and place cut side down on top of cream layer. Spread remaining whipped cream on top of torta and top with walnut halves. Refrigerate for at least 20 minutes but not more than 3 hours before serving. Just before serving, dust with confectioners' sugar.

Consider time when picking your main course. For a casual get-together on a weeknight, you will probably want a dish that is quickly and easily assembled, such as Linguine with Clams and Lemon. Or you may decide to celebrate the return to slow cooking with a leisurely Saturday supper featuring a festive crown roast of pork packed with a bread-and-mushroom stuffing. Main courses are also an excellent opportunity to think globally—to take your dinner guests on a gastronomic minitour to the continent. If you're pining for Paris, pick up the sauté pan and prepare chicken breasts with

morel-and-tarragon cream sauce. If you want to travel the world of seafood, cook up some Portuguese sardines with arugula (rocket) oil, Thai-style curried shrimp with coconut milk and kaffir lime leaves, a Provençal sea bass with a fragrant pistou, or an Italian seafood risotto.

Avoid choosing a main course that keeps you trapped in the kitchen once your guests have arrived. If the dish does demand last-minute attention, and your party is a casual affair, invite your guests to lend a hand with the finishing touches. A nice presentation is important, too. You can bring a whole roasted bird or fish to the table and carve or fillet it in front of your admiring guests. If being at center stage doesn't appeal, however, you can portion all the food in the kitchen, creating a beautifully composed plate to set before each diner.

Grilled Marinated Swordfish with Fresh Tomato Sauce

3 cloves garlic, coarsely chopped

4 large tomatoes (about 2 lb/1 kg), peeled, seeded, and diced

2 fresh bay leaves

3 tablespoons white wine vinegar

¼ cup (2 fl oz/60 ml) olive oil

sea salt and freshly ground black pepper

8 pieces swordfish (3 oz/90 g each), skin removed

SERVES 4

The fresh tomato sauce does double duty: After marinating and flavoring the swordfish, it's cooked down over high heat and served as an accompaniment, a strategy that works as well for many kinds of fish.

1 In a bowl, combine garlic, tomatoes, bay leaves, vinegar, and olive oil. Season to taste with salt and pepper. Put swordfish in a shallow dish and pour tomato mixture over. Cover and refrigerate for at least 30 minutes.

2 Preheat grill on high heat.

3 Remove swordfish from marinade, reserving marinade. Grill fish until just cooked through and opaque, about 5 minutes on each side.

4 Meanwhile, in a fireproof skillet placed on grill, bring reserved marinade to a simmer. Cook, stirring often, until sauce thickens, 5–6 minutes. Taste and adjust seasoning, if needed, with salt and pepper. Serve swordfish immediately with fresh tomato sauce alongside.

Thai Curried Shrimp with Kaffir Lime Leaves

1½ tablespoons peanut oil

¼ teaspoon coriander seeds

2 cloves garlic, finely chopped

1½ teaspoons grated peeled
fresh ginger

6 oz (185 g) shrimp (prawns), peeled
and deveined, tails intact

½ teaspoon ground cumin

1 large jalapeño chile, seeded and
finely chopped

3 kaffir lime leaves, finely chopped

1 tablespoon Thai fish sauce

1¾ cups (14 fl oz/430 ml) canned
coconut milk, whisked smooth

¼ cup (⅓ oz/10 g) chopped fresh
cilantro (fresh coriander) leaves

2 tablespoons fresh lime juice

lime wedges, for garnish

SERVES 2–3

Kaffir lime leaves and the gnarled fruit grown with them are a staple of Thai cooking. Their gentle tang is especially nice with sweet shrimp. Serve with steamed white rice.

1 Heat oil in a large sauté pan over high heat until it begins to smoke.

2 Add coriander seeds, stir, and lower heat to medium high. Stir in garlic and ginger. Add shrimp and cumin and sauté over medium heat until shrimp begin to turn pink around the edges, about 2 minutes.

3 Stir in jalapeño chile and lime leaves. Add fish sauce, stir, and add coconut milk. Bring mixture to a boil over medium-high heat. Lower heat to medium and simmer for 2 minutes. Stir in cilantro and lime juice and boil for 1 minute. Garnish with lime wedges and serve immediately.

Risotto with
Spring Vegetables

5½–6 cups (44–48 fl oz/1.35–1.5 l)
chicken or vegetable stock

3 tablespoons olive oil

1 shallot, finely chopped

1 clove garlic, finely chopped

1½ cups (10½ oz/330 g) Vialone Nano rice

½ cup (4 fl oz/125 ml) vermouth

½ cup (4 fl oz/125 ml) heavy cream

1½ cups (10 oz/315 g) fava beans, skinned

4 oz (125 g) asparagus, trimmed and cut
into 1-inch (2.5-cm) lengths

4 oz (125 g) baby zucchini, finely chopped

1 cup (3 oz/90 g) finely shredded spinach

salt and freshly ground black pepper

2 tablespoons butter

¾ cup (3 oz/90 g) grated Parmesan cheese

2 tablespoons finely chopped fresh basil

¼ cup (⅓ oz/10 g) finely chopped
fresh chervil

1 cup (5 oz/155 g) finely chopped wild
or baby fennel

2 tablespoons finely chopped fresh
flat-leaf (Italian) parsley

2 tablespoons finely chopped
fresh tarragon

SERVES 6

All the harbingers of spring are featured in this risotto: fava beans, asparagus, baby squash, and baby fennel. Serve as a vegetarian main course, or as a side dish with lamb or chicken.

1 In a saucepan, heat stock to a gentle simmer.

2 In a heavy-bottomed risotto pan or sauté pan over medium heat, warm olive oil. Stir in shallot and cook until shallot is translucent and soft, about 3 minutes. Stir in garlic and cook 1 minute longer. Add rice to pan and stir to coat. Cook until rice becomes slightly translucent and grains make a clicking noise. Add vermouth and stir until absorbed.

3 Start to add stock, a ladleful at a time, stirring constantly until all liquid is absorbed. After three-quarters of stock has been added, gradually stir in cream and vegetables; add spinach last, as it requires little cooking. Season to taste with salt and pepper; continue to add remaining stock. After a total of 20 minutes, rice should be al dente. Mixture should still be quite runny, or *all'onda,* in consistency.

4 Remove from heat and stir in butter, Parmesan cheese, and herbs. Cover pan and let rest about 3 minutes. Gently stir again. Add a little more stock if necessary to keep it quite loose, and adjust seasoning to taste. Serve immediately.

Linguine with Clams and Lemon

¼ cup (2 fl oz/60 ml) olive oil

1 clove garlic, finely chopped

2 lb (1 kg) Manila clams, scrubbed

⅓ cup (3 fl oz/80 ml) dry white wine

1 cup (8 fl oz/250 ml) fish stock or
bottled clam juice

1 lb (500 g) linguine

1 tablespoon grated lemon zest

freshly ground black pepper

SERVES 4

Every recipe for pasta with clam sauce varies a little—this one includes a judicious amount of tart lemon zest. If you like your pasta spicy, add a dash or two of crushed red pepper flakes.

1 In a large sauté pan, heat oil over medium-high heat. Add garlic and cook until fragrant, about 30 seconds. Discard any clams that do not close to the touch. Add clams, wine, and stock to sauté pan. Cover and cook until clams open, 4–5 minutes. Discard any clams that did not open.

2 Meanwhile, bring a large pot of salted water to a boil. Add pasta and cook until al dente, 8–10 minutes. Drain in a colander. Transfer pasta to a large warmed bowl and add clams and lemon zest. Season to taste with pepper and toss to combine.

Parisian Chicken Breasts with Morels and Tarragon

8 skinless, boneless chicken breasts

about 3 cups (24 fl oz/750 ml) chicken stock

1½ oz (45 g) dried morel mushrooms

2 tablespoons butter

2 shallots, finely chopped

2 tablespoons all-purpose (plain) flour

½ cup (4 fl oz/125 ml) heavy (double) cream

2 egg yolks

⅓ cup (½ oz/15 g) fresh tarragon leaves, chopped

kosher salt and freshly ground white pepper

SERVES 8

Morel mushrooms and herbed cream sauce are a sublime combination. Spoon over poached chicken breasts—the result is a dish that's both comforting and luxurious.

1 In a 12-inch (30-cm) sauté pan, arrange chicken breasts with thin points in center. Pour in chicken stock to cover. Bring to a boil, shifting chicken pieces occasionally to prevent sticking. Lower heat to a simmer and cook for 3 minutes. Turn chicken pieces over and continue to simmer until just cooked through, about 3 minutes longer.

2 Transfer chicken to a plate. Set aside and keep warm. Transfer stock to a saucepan and bring to a boil. Add morel mushrooms and cook for 2 minutes. Skim out morels, roughly chopping large ones, and set aside. Strain stock through a sieve lined with dampened cheesecloth (muslin) or a coffee filter. Rinse saucepan, then return strained stock to it and boil until reduced to 2 cups (16 fl oz/500 ml), 8–10 minutes.

3 Meanwhile, heat 1 tablespoon butter in a skillet over medium-low heat. Add morels and cook, stirring often, until tender, 5–6 minutes. Set aside and keep warm.

4 In a large saucepan, melt remaining 1 tablespoon butter over medium-low heat. Add shallots and cook until translucent, 3–4 minutes. Stir in flour; cook 2 minutes longer.

5 Add reduced stock and cook, whisking, over medium heat until thickened. Stir in cream and lower heat to low.

6 In a small bowl, whisk egg yolks. Slowly whisk 1 cup (8 fl oz/250 ml) sauce into egg yolks, then whisk egg yolk mixture into remaining sauce. Stir in tarragon and morels. Season to taste with kosher salt and white pepper. Add chicken pieces and reheat gently. Do not allow sauce to boil.

7 To serve, thickly slice each chicken breast, place on a serving plate, and top with sauce.

Pan-Roasted Chicken
with Apple-Fennel Slaw

5 tablespoons (2½ fl oz/75 ml)
canola oil

½ lb (250 g) fresh chanterelle or
hedgehog mushrooms, wiped clean
and quartered

salt and freshly ground black pepper

½ cup (4 fl oz/125 ml) dry
white wine

½ cup (4 oz/125 g) whole-grain
mustard

1 cup (8 fl oz/250 ml) chicken stock

1 large fennel bulb, halved, cored, and
thinly sliced crosswise

1 tart apple, quartered, cored, and
thinly sliced

juice of 1 lemon

1 tablespoon extra-virgin olive oil

4 chicken breasts (½ lb/250 g each)

SERVES 4

The spectacular Sierra Mar restaurant stands over the Pacific in Big Sur. There, chef Craig von Foerester makes simple but delicious dishes, like chicken on a bed of sliced fennel and apple, which can be served any time of year.

1 Preheat oven to 350°F (180°C).

2 In a skillet, heat 2 tablespoons canola oil over medium-high heat. Add mushrooms and sauté, stirring occasionally, until lightly browned, about 5 minutes. Season to taste with salt and pepper and drain off any excess liquid. Add wine and cook until evaporated. Add mustard and chicken stock and simmer until reduced by one-fourth. Season to taste with salt and pepper. Set aside and keep warm.

3 In a bowl, combine sliced fennel and apple. Drizzle with lemon juice and olive oil and toss to coat. Season to taste with salt and pepper.

4 In a heavy ovenproof skillet, heat remaining 3 tablespoons canola oil over medium heat. Season chicken to taste with salt and pepper. Place skin side down in skillet and cook until browned, about 5 minutes. Turn and cook for 5 minutes longer. Turn again and transfer skillet to oven. Roast chicken until browned and crisp, 5–8 minutes. Remove from oven and let stand for 5 minutes.

5 Mound apple-fennel salad on 4 large plates and set a chicken breast on top. Spoon mustard sauce around chicken.

Asparagus

wild nettle ravioli

NETTLES
FARMSTAND

FRESH ORGANIC
PASTA
VEGETABLES
EGGS
CHICKENS

DAILY 9-6
758-7616

Herb Nettle Ravioli

PASTA

6 oz (185 g) nettle or spinach leaves, stemmed
and rinsed

1 egg, lightly beaten

½ teaspoon sea salt

2 cups (10 oz/315 g) all-purpose (plain) flour,
plus more if needed

FILLING

1½ cups (12 oz/375 g) ricotta cheese, preferably
whole-milk ricotta

¼ cup (1 oz/30 g) freshly grated
Parmigiano-Reggiano cheese, plus cheese
shavings for garnish

¼ cup (1 oz/30 g) freshly grated pecorino
Romano cheese

1 egg, lightly beaten

½ cup (¾ oz/20 g) finely chopped fresh
flat-leaf (Italian) parsley

½ cup (¾ oz/20 g) minced fresh chives

salt and freshly ground white pepper

rice flour, for sprinkling

NETTLE BROTH

5 tablespoons (2½ oz/75 g) butter

1 tablespoon extra-virgin olive oil

6 oz (185 g) nettle or spinach leaves, stemmed

1 cup (8 fl oz/250 ml) chicken stock or water

salt

SERVES 4–5

1 FOR PASTA: Using tongs, plunge nettle or spinach leaves into a large pot of boiling, salted water. Drain as soon as wilted and dark, bright green. Press out excess moisture. Finely chop greens. In a bowl, combine greens, egg, and sea salt.

2 On a work surface, mound 2 cups (10 oz/315 g) flour, make a well in center, and pour in greens mixture. Using your fingers, drag in flour from edges to combine. When all flour has been combined, begin to work it into a unified mass. The texture should be slightly dry. If it seems too dry, add a few drops water. If too sticky, work in a little more flour. Knead until dough is silky, about 15 minutes. Cover with a bowl or plastic wrap and let rest for 45 minutes.

3 FOR FILLING: While pasta is resting, combine 3 cheeses with egg in a bowl. Stir in parsley and chives. Season to taste with salt and white pepper. Set aside.

4 Divide dough into 4 equal pieces and roll out each on a pasta machine, ending with finest or next-to-last setting. Dough must be thin, but not too thin to hold filling; each sheet will be about 18 inches (45 cm) long. Trim edges and lay sheets on a counter sprinkled with rice flour. Working with 1 sheet at a time, fold lightly lengthwise to make a center crease and open again. Drop teaspoonfuls of filling every 3 inches (7.5 cm) down center of one half. Fold other half of dough over mounds and press firmly around filling with your fingers to seal. Using a ravioli or pastry cutter, cut into squares. Put them on baking sheets sprinkled with rice flour. Repeat with rest of dough for 20 ravioli total. Bring a large pot of salted water to a boil.

5 FOR NETTLE BROTH: In a wide skillet, heat butter and oil. Add nettle or spinach leaves and pour in stock or water. Simmer until greens are tender. Drain, season to taste with salt, and divide among shallow individual bowls.

6 Lower heat for pasta water to a slow boil. Add ravioli and cook until tender, about 2 minutes. Transfer to bowls and garnish with shavings of Parmigiano-Reggiano.

Cheese Grits with Shrimp and Mushrooms

CHEESE GRITS

1 cup (6 oz/185 g) stone-ground grits

1 teaspoon salt

½ cup (2 oz/60 g) shredded sharp cheddar cheese

½ cup (2 oz/60 g) freshly grated Parmesan cheese

3 tablespoons butter

freshly ground black pepper

Tabasco or other hot-pepper sauce

SHRIMP TOPPING

3 slices bacon, chopped

1 lb (500 g) shrimp (prawns), peeled and deveined

2 tablespoons all-purpose (plain) flour

2 tablespoons peanut oil

1¼ cups (4 oz/125 g) sliced white mushrooms

1 large clove garlic, finely chopped with a pinch of salt to form a paste

Tabasco or other hot-pepper sauce

2 teaspoons fresh lemon juice

salt

½ cup (1½ oz/45 g) thinly sliced green (spring) onions, including pale green tops

SERVES 4

Grits are made from hominy, dried hulled corn kernels. A Southern institution, grits are served at breakfast and throughout the day as part of a main course. The addition of mushrooms to this low-country shrimp classic is the inspiration of Robert Stehling at Hominy Diner in Charleston.

1 FOR CHEESE GRITS: In a saucepan, bring 4½ cups (36 fl oz/1.1 l) water to a boil. Quickly whisk in grits and salt, lower heat to a simmer, and cook until water is absorbed, 35–40 minutes. Remove from heat and stir in cheeses and butter until melted. Season to taste with pepper and Tabasco.

2 FOR SHRIMP TOPPING: Meanwhile, in a large skillet, fry bacon in its own fat until crisp, 5–8 minutes. Transfer bacon to paper towels to drain. Pour off all but 1 tablespoon of bacon fat in pan.

3 In a bowl, gently toss shrimp with flour until lightly coated. Discard excess flour. Add peanut oil to pan with bacon fat and heat over medium-high heat. Add shrimp and sauté until partially cooked, 1–2 minutes. Add mushrooms and toss to coat. When mushrooms begin to cook, stir in reserved bacon, then quickly stir in garlic paste, Tabasco to taste, and lemon juice. Do not let garlic brown. Cook until shrimp are opaque and cooked through and mushrooms are golden brown, 2–3 minutes longer.

4 Season to taste with salt. Add green onions, stir, and remove from heat. Spoon shrimp mixture over cheese grits. Serve immediately.

Stuffed Breast of Veal

STUFFING

2 tablespoons unsalted butter

½ onion, chopped

1 clove garlic, chopped

1 lb (500 g) ground (minced) pork

½ lb (250 g) peeled roasted chestnuts, chopped

1 tablespoon chopped fresh flat-leaf (Italian) parsley

¼ teaspoon ground cloves

¼ teaspoon dried sage

¼ teaspoon freshly ground black pepper

1 teaspoon salt

1 breast of veal (2½ lb/1.25 kg), with a pocket cut into it

1 tablespoon unsalted butter, softened

salt and freshly ground black pepper

½ onion, coarsely chopped

2 carrots, peeled and coarsely chopped

½ lb (250 g) peeled roasted chestnuts, halved

5 fresh parsley stems, tied together with kitchen string

1 bay leaf

1 cup (8 fl oz/250 ml) dry white wine

SERVES 6

Chopped chestnuts hidden in the tender veal infuse it with sweetness. If you can't find fresh chestnuts, substitute vacuum-packed. Fran Gage advises against using canned chestnuts preserved in water, which fall apart during cooking.

1 Preheat oven to 475°F (245°C).

2 FOR STUFFING: In a skillet, melt butter over medium heat. Sauté onion and garlic until soft but not browned, about 8 minutes. In a bowl, combine sautéed onion and garlic, ground pork, chestnuts, parsley, cloves, sage, pepper, and salt and mix well.

3 Distribute stuffing evenly in pocket of veal. Rub top of meat with butter and sprinkle to taste with salt and pepper. Put meat in a Dutch oven or roasting pan. Roast for 10 minutes.

4 Add onion and carrots to pan and roast for 10 minutes longer. Remove pan from oven and lower oven temperature to 350°F (180°C). Add chestnuts, parsley stems, bay leaf, wine, and 1 cup (8 fl oz/250 ml) water to pan. Bring to a boil over medium-high heat on stove top. Cover with a lid or aluminum foil and return to oven.

5 Cook veal until an instant-read thermometer inserted in stuffing reaches 170°F (77°C), about 1 hour. Transfer to a platter and let stand for 15 minutes.

6 Discard parsley stems and bay leaf. Pour pan liquid into a glass measuring pitcher, reserving vegetables. Refrigerate liquid for 10 minutes. Discard fat that rises to top. Pour liquid into a saucepan and boil over high heat to reduce by one-third, about 5 minutes. Return vegetables to reduced sauce.

7 Slice veal between ribs and serve with cooked vegetables and sauce.

Jerked Bluefish with Plantain and Purple Potato Chips

1 lb (500 g) skinned bluefish fillet, cut into 1-inch (2.5-cm) cubes

¼ cup (2 fl oz/60 ml) olive oil

1½ tablespoons jerk sauce

canola oil, for frying

2 green plantains (about ½ lb/250 g)

2 large purple potatoes (about ½ lb/250 g)

salt

1 lime, cut into wedges

SERVES 4

This is the perfect dish to start a party whether you're by the pool or the ocean, or wishing that you were. Homemade plantain and potato chips are especially nice, but they can be replaced by store-bought ones if you're short on time.

1 In a bowl, toss bluefish cubes with olive oil and jerk sauce. Cover and marinate in refrigerator for up to 2 hours.

2 In a deep fryer, heat canola oil to 375°F (190°C) on a deep-frying thermometer.

3 Score skin of plantains and dip in hot tap water until skin loosens, about 5 minutes. Pat dry, peel, and cut in half crosswise. Using a mandoline, thinly cut plantains lengthwise into slices ⅛ inch (3 mm) thick. Working in small batches, fry until crisp and just beginning to brown, 2–3 minutes. Drain on paper towels and sprinkle with salt. Oil should be 375°F (190°C) before continuing with next batch.

4 Peel purple potatoes, slice, and fry in batches as above, 3–4 minutes. Drain on paper towels and sprinkle with salt.

5 Preheat grill on high heat.

6 Grill bluefish cubes, turning occasionally, until cooked through, about 5 minutes. Serve with plantain chips, potato chips, and lime wedges.

Gala Crown Roast of Pork

1 crown roast of pork (about 9½ lbs/
4.75 kg and 9½ inches/24 cm in
diameter), formed from 2 racks of
8 or 9 chops each, all fat removed,
bones frenched, cut apart at chine
end to facilitate carving

4 oz (125 g) dried morel mushrooms

1 oz (30 g) dried porcini
mushroom slices

1 oz (30 g) dried oyster
mushroom slices

1 tablespoon butter

1 yellow onion, diced

⅓ cup (½ oz/15 g) chopped fresh
flat-leaf (Italian) parsley

1 tablespoon chopped fresh
sage leaves

1 tablespoon kosher salt

freshly ground black pepper

¼ lb (125 g) sourdough rye bread,
cut in ½-inch (12-mm) cubes
(about 1¼ cups)

½ teaspoon caraway seeds, if bread
is seedless

1 cup (8 fl oz/250 ml) chicken stock

SERVES 8–10

1 Place pork in a roasting pan and wrap a band of aluminum foil around exposed bone to prevent charring.

2 In a saucepan, bring 2 cups (16 fl oz/500 ml) water to a boil. Add morel mushrooms and cook for 2 minutes. Transfer morels to a bowl. Line a sieve with dampened cheesecloth (muslin) and strain morel liquid. Rinse saucepan and return morel liquid to it. Add enough water to make 4 cups (32 fl oz/ 1 l). Bring to a boil, add porcini and oyster mushrooms, and cook for 2 minutes. Transfer mushrooms to a small bowl. Reserve liquid in pan. Using a slotted spoon, press down hard on reserved mushrooms to extract accumulated juices and add to mushroom cooking liquid. Cook over medium-high heat until reduced to ¾ cup (6 fl oz/180 ml).

3 Put a rack in second position from oven bottom and preheat oven to 550°F (290°C).

4 In a saucepan, melt butter over medium-low heat. Add onion and sauté until translucent, 5 minutes. Coarsely chop morel, porcini, and oyster mushrooms. In a bowl, combine sautéed onion, mushrooms, parsley, sage, kosher salt, pepper to taste, bread cubes, caraway seeds, and reduced mushroom liquid.

5 Pile as much stuffing into roast as possible, pressing and mounding mixture. Reserve remaining stuffing. Butter a small piece of foil and use to cover stuffing in roast. Roast for 40 minutes. Remove foil. Continue roasting until meat reaches 145°F (63°C) on an instant-read thermometer inserted in thickest part of meat away from bone, about 10 minutes longer. Protecting hands with oven mitts, transfer roast to a warmed platter and discard aluminum foil on bones. Tent loosely with more foil and let stand for 30 minutes.

6 Meanwhile, place roasting pan on stove top over medium heat. Add stock and 1 cup (8 fl oz/250 ml) water and bring to boil, scraping pan to dissolve meat juices. Transfer liquid to saucepan and add reserved stuffing. Simmer until mush-rooms are cooked and sauce is thickened, about 10 minutes.

7 Separate roast into chops. Serve with stuffing and sauce.

Grilled Mahi Mahi with Baby Vegetables

¾ cup (6 fl oz/180 ml) olive oil

1 tablespoon mixed dry herbs such as fennel, thyme, dill, and crumbled bay leaf

4 pieces mahi mahi (6 oz/185 g each)

8 baby artichokes

1 lemon

8 baby golden beets, greens trimmed

4 cloves garlic, lightly smashed

1 jalapeño chile, seeded and cut into thin strips

2 fresh bay leaves

¼ teaspoon whole black peppercorns

¼ teaspoon whole coriander seeds

3 dried oregano sprigs

3 fresh thyme sprigs

1 tablespoon sea salt

8 heads baby fennel, trimmed

6 oz (185 g) red pearl onions

12 baby carrots, trimmed and peeled

½ cup (4 fl oz/125 ml) red or white wine vinegar

1 cup (8 fl oz/250 ml) dry white wine

salt and freshly ground black pepper

SERVES 4

This colorful spring dish makes a lovely presentation. Mahi mahi, a versatile, firm, white fish, takes particularly well to grilling. If unavailable, substitute another firm fish, such as halibut.

1 In a small bowl, combine ¼ cup (2 fl oz/60 ml) olive oil and dried herbs. Put mahi mahi in a shallow dish and pour oil mixture over. Cover and refrigerate for 30 minutes.

2 Peel off tough outer leaves from baby artichokes and cut off top third and discard. Peel and trim stems and discard. Put trimmed artichokes in a bowl with water to cover and juice of 1 lemon.

3 In a saucepan, cover beets with water and bring to a boil over high heat. Lower heat to a simmer and cook until tender, about 12 minutes. Drain and let cool slightly. Peel beets and set aside.

4 In a saucepan, cover artichokes with water and bring to a boil over high heat. Lower heat to a simmer and cook until tender when pierced with a knife, about 5 minutes. Drain and let cool.

5 In a large sauté pan, heat ¼ cup (2 fl oz/60 ml) olive oil and garlic over medium heat. Add jalapeño chile, bay leaves, peppercorns, coriander seeds, oregano, thyme, and sea salt. Sauté until fragrant, about 1 minute. Add fennel, pearl onions, and carrots and sauté for about 3 minutes. Add remaining ¼ cup (2 fl oz/60 ml) olive oil, vinegar, and wine and simmer for 5 minutes. Remove from heat and let cool to room temperature in broth.

6 Preheat grill on medium-high heat.

7 Season fish to taste with salt and pepper. Grill until just cooked through, 4–5 minutes on each side. Serve immediately with baby vegetables and stock.

Grilled Sardines with Arugula Oil

2 bunches arugula (rocket) (about 1 lb/500 g)

2 teaspoons fresh lemon juice

sea salt and freshly ground black pepper

1 cup (8 fl oz/250 ml) extra-virgin olive oil, plus more for brushing

12 fresh sardines, scaled and gutted

SERVES 4

Sardines are a staple of the Mediterranean grilling repertoire, especially in Portugal, where every family has an individual sardine grill. This recipe captures the Portuguese spirit.

1 In a large saucepan of salted boiling water, cook arugula until just wilted, about 30 seconds. Plunge into a bowl of ice water to halt cooking. Drain and squeeze out all water from arugula.

2 In a food processor, combine arugula and lemon juice and season to taste with salt and pepper. Purée and, with machine running, slowly add olive oil in a thin, steady stream. Pour into a small bowl and let stand 30 minutes at room temperature.

3 Season sardines to taste with salt. Cover and refrigerate for 30 minutes.

4 Strain arugula oil through a sieve lined with cheesecloth (muslin) set over a bowl. Gently wring cheesecloth and discard solids. Set arugula oil aside.

5 Preheat grill on medium-high heat.

6 Brush sardines with olive oil. Grill until cooked through, 2–3 minutes on each side. Serve immediately with arugula oil.

Woodcutter's Lamb

4 lb (2 kg) young lamb, including
6 loin chops and 8 rib chops, cut into
3-inch (7.5-cm) chunks, about 1 inch
(2.5 cm) thick, bones included

½ cup (4 fl oz/125 ml) extra-virgin
olive oil, plus 2 tablespoons

¼ cup (⅓ oz/10 g) coarsely chopped
fresh flat-leaf (Italian) parsley

4 or 5 fresh bay leaves

leaves from 2 fresh rosemary sprigs,
roughly chopped

2 stalks celery, cut into 1-inch
(2.5-cm) pieces

2 tablespoons balsamic vinegar

2 lemons, cut into wedges

2½ lb (1.25 kg) large new potatoes
(about 10–12), peeled and cut into
2-inch (5-cm) strips, about 1 inch
(2.5 cm) thick

sea salt

3 tablespoons chopped fresh oregano

SERVES 6

Chef Bobo Vicenzi owns a fish restaurant near Italy's Adriatic coast, but he loves roasting meat. He bakes this dish in the hot ashes of a fireplace, although a hot oven works well, too. He recommends putting a pan of water in the oven to counteract its dry heat.

1 In a very large bowl, combine lamb with ½ cup olive oil, parsley, bay leaves, rosemary, celery, balsamic vinegar, and lemon wedges. Toss together. Cover with plastic wrap and refrigerate overnight or up to 24 hours, stirring once or twice.

2 Preheat oven to 500°F (260°C). Fill a small roasting pan halfway with water; place on oven floor, below bottom rack.

3 Spread half of potatoes in a large heavy ovenproof casserole with lid. Sprinkle generously with sea salt and 1 tablespoon oregano. Remove lamb from marinade and transfer to casserole, on top of potatoes. Season with sea salt and another 1 tablespoon oregano. Top with remaining potatoes and season generously with sea salt and with remaining oregano. Drizzle with remaining 2 tablespoons olive oil.

4 Cover and roast until starting to simmer, about 20 minutes. Remove pan from oven and carefully pour out and discard liquid. Return pan to oven, uncovered. Continue to roast, stirring occasionally, until lamb is browned and tender and potatoes are lightly golden, about 45 minutes.

Grilled Soft-Shell Crabs
with Samphire Salad

2 oz (60 g) samphire

2 avocados

4 oz (125 g) jicama, peeled and thinly sliced

2 oranges, peeled and cut into segments

Olivado extra-virgin avocado oil for drizzling, plus ¼ cup (2 fl oz/60 ml) for brushing

salt and freshly ground black pepper

8 soft-shell crabs, cleaned

SERVES 4

Samphire, also known as sea beans or glasswort, is a sea vegetable that retains its oceanlike taste. If unavailable, an attractive substitute is watercress. Delicate extra-virgin avocado oil flavors both the crabs and salad in this dish. If you can't locate this particular oil, use a good-quality extra-virgin olive oil in its place.

1 Preheat grill on high heat.

2 In a saucepan of boiling water, blanch samphire for about 30 seconds. Drain and plunge into a bowl filled with ice water to stop cooking. Drain again and set aside.

3 Peel and dice avocados. In a large bowl, combine jicama, avocados, orange segments, and samphire. Drizzle with avocado oil and season to taste with salt and pepper. Toss gently. Set aside.

4 Brush crabs with ¼ cup avocado oil and season to taste with salt and pepper. Grill, turning occasionally, until bright orange, 2–3 minutes on each side. Serve immediately with salad.

Peel-and-Eat
Spot Prawns

Prawns are a name often used interchangeably with shrimp, although true prawns are red and look like miniature lobsters. Spot prawns are a West Coast shellfish, but if they're unavailable, you can substitute medium-sized shrimp in this recipe from Deborah Madison.

SALSA

½ cup (¾ oz/20 g) finely chopped fresh flat-leaf (Italian) parsley

¼ cup (⅓ oz/10 g) finely chopped fresh lovage or celery leaves

1 large shallot, finely diced

½ cup (4 fl oz/125 ml) extra-virgin olive oil

½ teaspoon sea salt

grated zest and juice of 1 lemon

2 tablespoons olive oil

1 lb (500 g) spot prawns (about 20–25), with shells and heads intact, if desired

sea salt

2 cloves garlic, chopped

SERVES 2–4

1 FOR SALSA: In a bowl, combine parsley, lovage or celery leaves, shallot, extra-virgin olive oil, sea salt, and lemon zest. Stir in lemon juice to taste. Set aside.

2 In a wide skillet, heat olive oil over medium-high heat. When oil is hot, add spot prawns, sprinkle generously with sea salt, and sauté until red on both sides, about 2 minutes. Add ¼ cup (2 fl oz/60 ml) water and garlic. Cook for 2–3 minutes longer, and then transfer spot prawns to a serving bowl.

3 Serve immediately with salsa.

Tuna Niçoise Sandwiches with Caperberries

The ingredients of a top-notch niçoise salad are deconstructed and layered between a halved baguette. This sandwich is both sophisticated and playful—wonderful for almost any lunch. Don't overcook the tuna or the sandwich will be dry.

SALAD

6 small waxy potatoes

½ lb (250 g) yellow wax beans or haricots verts, trimmed

8 anchovy fillets

1 red onion, thinly sliced

8 caperberries

¼ cup (1 oz/30 g) niçoise or kalamata olives

4½ teaspoons white wine vinegar

3 tablespoons extra-virgin olive oil

salt and freshly ground black pepper

SANDWICHES

¼ cup (2 fl oz/60 ml) olive oil, plus 1 tablespoon

1 tablespoon coarsely chopped fresh rosemary

4 pieces fresh tuna (5 oz/155 g each), about 1 inch (2.5 cm) thick

1 French baguette, sliced horizontally and then cut crosswise into 4 pieces

1 large clove garlic, halved, for rubbing bread

2 tomatoes, cored and thinly sliced

2 hard-boiled eggs, thinly sliced

SERVES 4

1 FOR SALAD: In a saucepan, cover potatoes with salted water and bring to a boil over high heat. Lower heat to a simmer and cook until tender when pierced with a knife, about 15 minutes. Drain and let cool. Slice potatoes into thin rounds.

2 In a saucepan of salted boiling water, cook beans until crisp-tender, 2–3 minutes. Plunge into a bowl of ice water to stop cooking. Drain and set aside.

3 In a large serving bowl, combine sliced potatoes, beans, anchovies, onion slices, caperberries, and olives.

4 In a small bowl, whisk together vinegar and olive oil and season to taste with salt and pepper. Set dressing aside.

5 FOR SANDWICHES: Preheat grill on high heat.

6 In a small bowl, combine ¼ cup (2 fl oz/60 ml) olive oil and rosemary. Put tuna in a shallow dish and pour oil mixture over. Cover and refrigerate for 30 minutes.

7 Remove tuna from marinade and season to taste with salt and pepper. Grill fish until medium-rare, 1–2 minutes on each side.

8 Lightly brush cut sides of bread with remaining 1 tablespoon olive oil. Grill, cut sides down, until lightly browned, 30–45 seconds. Lightly rub grilled bread with garlic halves.

9 Arrange tuna on each of 4 bread halves, top with tomato slices, egg slices, and remaining bread halves. Drizzle salad with dressing and serve alongside sandwiches.

Side dishes are typically defined as accompaniments to the main course, but that simple description fails to convey the indispensable role these preparations play. A side dish is often both the spark of creativity and the swatch of color on a plate—the critical element that gives visual interest to a plain grilled fish fillet or a pan-seared veal chop. It is typically based on vegetables or grains, but it can assume any number of guises, from a sauté to a braise to a gratin to a roast. And while the side dish is perfectly suited to its supporting role, it can also be offered in a larger portion, to star in place of the main course.

Savvy hosts select their sides according to the season. In autumn, carrots, broccoli, and tiny onions are deep roasted to bring out their natural flavors. Spring is the time for bright green asparagus, here drizzled with a citrus-rosemary butter. The same months also bring tender, young garden peas, which are delicious married with shredded lettuce and fresh mint. Young greens, preferably wild, need nothing more than the classic Italian treatment of boiling until tender and then serving with a

splash of olive oil and a squeeze of lemon juice. If these dishes all sound surprisingly easy, it's because they are. The best sides are invariably the simplest preparations.

If you are planning to serve two or more side dishes, select recipes that call for different cooking methods to shorten your time at the stove. For example, assemble a menu that has one side dish baking in the oven, another simmering on the stove top, and a third already prepared and ready to serve at room temperature. Keep color in mind, too, placing deep red baked tomatoes alongside a grilled swordfish steak, or bright orange pickled carrots next to a poached chicken breast.

Baked Tomatoes with Green Rice

1 cup (7 oz/220 g) white rice

1¼ teaspoons salt

½ cup (2½ oz/75 g) pine nuts

4 cloves garlic, coarsely chopped

1 cup (1½ oz/45 g) packed, finely chopped fresh cilantro (fresh coriander), including leaves and stems

⅓ cup (½ oz/15 g) finely chopped fresh flat-leaf (Italian) parsley

1½ teaspoons sweet paprika

1 teaspoon ground cumin

⅛ teaspoon cayenne pepper

⅓ cup (3 fl oz/80 ml) extra-virgin olive oil, plus more for brushing tomato lids

3 tablespoons fresh lemon juice

8 tomatoes (about 5–6 oz/ 155–185 g each)

SERVES 8

Baked tomatoes are usually a cold-weather standby, made with the off-season, hard-as-a-rock variety. Deborah Madison seeks out wonderful tomatoes and uses an assortment of herbs in her stuffing to make this a colorful dish that can be served as either an accompaniment or as a first course.

1 In a saucepan, bring 4 cups (32 fl oz/1 l) water to a boil. Add rice and ½ teaspoon salt. Lower heat slightly to achieve a simmer and cook until rice is tender, about 15 minutes. Remove from heat and drain in a large sieve. Rinse with cold water to stop cooking.

2 Meanwhile, in a dry skillet, toast pine nuts over medium-high heat, tossing until pale gold, about 5 minutes. Remove from heat and pour onto a plate to let cool. Set aside.

3 In bowl of a food processor, combine garlic, cilantro, parsley, paprika, cumin, cayenne, remaining ¾ teaspoon salt, olive oil, and lemon juice. Pulse until a coarse purée is formed. Reserve 1 tablespoon purée and set aside. In a bowl, toss remaining purée with rice and add all but 3 tablespoons of toasted pine nuts.

4 Preheat oven to 400°F (200°C). Lightly oil a baking dish that is just large enough to hold the tomatoes in a single layer. Slice top quarter off tomatoes and set aside. Using a spoon, scoop out pulp and seeds from each tomato and discard, leaving a wall at least ⅓ inch (9 mm) thick. Fill tomatoes with rice mixture and top with remaining pine nuts.

5 Brush tomato lids with olive oil and place on top of each tomato. Bake until tomatoes are tender and stuffing is hot, about 25 minutes. Brush reserved purée over tomatoes. Let cool to room temperature before serving.

Deep-Roasted
Fall Vegetables

1 lb (500 g) small white onions, about 1¼ inches (3 cm) in diameter

3 tablespoons olive oil

½ lb (250 g) carrots, peeled and cut crosswise into 1-inch (2.5-cm) slices

½ lb (250 g) broccoli florets

1 lb (500 g) yellow summer squash, quartered lengthwise and cut into 1-inch (2.5-cm) pieces

2 tablespoons finely chopped fresh marjoram

kosher salt and freshly ground black pepper

SERVES 4–6

Use Barbara Kafka's recipe as a guide to experiment with other vegetables. You can also substitute other fresh herbs—alone or in combination—for the marjoram. The dish works well for almost any kind of dinner party, whether served hot as a side dish with simple roasted meats or as a light vegetarian main course, or cooled and lightly dressed with a little more olive oil and some balsamic vinegar.

1 To peel onions, trim off top and root ends and make a small X in each root end. Drop into a pot of boiling water. When it returns to a boil, drain onions, plunge into cold water, and drain again. Slip off skins.

2 Place a rack at lowest level of oven and preheat oven to 500°F (260°C). Coat bottom of a heavy 18-by-13-inch (45-by-33-cm) roasting pan with olive oil. Add onions and shake pan to coat them with oil. Roast for 7 minutes.

3 Shake pan to turn onions over. Move them to center of pan. Surround onions with carrots, broccoli, and squash. Roast for 15 minutes.

4 Turn vegetables over. Roast until browned and tender, about 7 minutes.

5 Sprinkle evenly with marjoram and roast for 3 minutes longer.

6 Season to taste with salt and pepper. Serve hot.

Peas with Mint

¼ cup (2 oz/60 g) unsalted
butter

2 cups (10 oz/315 g) shelled fresh
peas (about 1½ lb/750 g in the shell)
or frozen peas

¼ cup (⅓ oz/10 g) packed mint
leaves, julienned

1½ cups (4 oz/125 g) julienned
butter (Boston) lettuce leaves, plus
several whole inner leaves

¼ teaspoon kosher salt

½ teaspoon sugar

SERVES 2

Peas—a sweetly starchy legume—pair beautifully with butter in this classic French dish. The nearly identical Italian preparation, *piselli alla romana,* is made with olive oil and prosciutto.

1 In a small pan, melt butter over medium heat. Add peas and cook for about 2 minutes. Cover and cook until peas are just tender, 3–5 minutes. Stir in mint and cook for 2 minutes longer. Add lettuce strips and cook until lettuce has wilted, 2–3 minutes.

2 Remove from heat, quickly stir in whole lettuce leaves to wilt slightly, and add salt and sugar. Serve immediately.

Risotto Milanese

5–6 cups (40–48 fl oz/1.25–1.5 l) chicken stock

1 teaspoon lightly packed saffron threads

3 tablespoons olive oil

2½ oz (75 g) finely diced pancetta

2 shallots, finely chopped

1½ cups (10½ oz/330 g) Arborio rice

½ cup (4 fl oz/125 ml) dry white wine

salt and freshly ground black pepper

3 tablespoons unsalted butter, softened

½ cup (2 oz/60 g) freshly grated Parmesan cheese, plus more for serving

SERVES 4

The traditional accompaniment to osso buco, Risotto Milanese is also lovely served with veal chops. The addition of saffron makes the risotto luxurious—perfect for a special occasion.

1 In a saucepan over medium heat, heat stock to a gentle simmer. In a small bowl, soak saffron in ¼ cup (2 fl oz/60 ml) hot water. Set aside.

2 In a heavy-bottomed risotto pan or sauté pan over medium heat, warm olive oil. Stir in pancetta and cook for 2 minutes, then stir in shallots. Cook until shallots are translucent and soft, 3–4 minutes.

3 Add rice to pan and stir to coat. Cook until rice becomes slightly translucent and grains make a clicking noise that indicates rice has absorbed all oil.

4 Quickly add wine, stirring constantly. Cook just until liquid is absorbed, about 1 minute.

5 Start to add stock a ladleful at a time, stirring well between each addition, and adding next ladleful only when previous stock is absorbed. Maintain heat at medium level: If too high, liquid will evaporate rather than be absorbed by rice; if too low, rice will become mushy. Stir gently every 2–3 minutes with a wooden spoon. Vigorous stirring can cause rice to become gluey; too little stirring will make it watery. When half of stock has been added, stir in saffron mixture and season to taste with salt and pepper.

6 After about 15 minutes of adding stock (using about three-fourths of it), liquid in pan will become increasingly viscous. Add stock in smaller amounts to avoid overcooking. Keep tasting; when done, rice should be al dente. Final mixture will have a thick, creamy consistency.

7 Remove from heat and stir in butter and Parmesan cheese. Taste and adjust seasoning, if needed, with salt and pepper. Cover and let rest for 3 minutes. Stir again and serve immediately with more Parmesan cheese.

Artichokes a la Polita

juice of 2 lemons

4 large artichokes, long stems intact

⅓ cup (3 fl oz/80 ml) extra-virgin
olive oil

2 cups (16 fl oz/500 ml) vegetable or
chicken stock

¾ lb (12 oz/375 g) small new
potatoes or waxy potatoes, peeled
and halved

3 carrots, peeled and cut into 2-inch
(5-cm) lengths, about ½ inch
(12 mm) thick

½ lb (250 g) pearl onions

salt and freshly ground black pepper

2 teaspoons finely chopped fresh dill

SERVES 4

This Greek dish makes a wonderful side dish or vegetarian meal. It can be served hot, warm, or cool, with a chunk of feta cheese and crusty bread.

1 Fill a large bowl with cold water and juice from 1 lemon. Working with 1 artichoke at a time, trim tip of stem, leaving long stem attached. Cut off top of artichoke down to level of heart. Break off and discard all leaves. Peel stem and pare leaf ends down to heart. Scoop out choke with a sharp spoon. Submerge artichoke in lemon water to prevent discoloring while you prepare remaining artichokes.

2 Drain artichokes and pat dry with paper towels. In a large saucepan, heat olive oil over high heat. Add artichokes, stems laid flat, and sauté, turning frequently for an even golden color, about 5 minutes. Add stock and extra water, if needed, to cover artichokes. Add remaining lemon juice and bring to a boil, then lower heat to a simmer. Cover and cook for 15 minutes.

3 Add potatoes, carrots, and pearl onions. Season to taste with salt and pepper. Continue to simmer until artichokes, potatoes, and carrots are tender, 20 minutes longer.

4 The cooking liquid should be reduced and syrupy. If not, gently transfer artichokes and vegetables to a serving bowl or platter, leaving cooking liquid in pan. Reduce over high heat until you have about ¾ cup (6 fl oz/180 ml) sauce, 2–3 minutes. Pour sauce over artichokes and vegetables and sprinkle with dill.

Roasted Asparagus with Citrus-Rosemary Butter

2 lb (1 kg) asparagus with thick
stalks

1 teaspoon olive oil

sea salt

¼ cup (2 oz/60 ml) fresh lemon
or orange juice

3 tablespoons cold butter,
cut into chunks

1 teaspoon grated lemon zest

2 teaspoons finely chopped fresh
rosemary

freshly ground black pepper

SERVES 4–6

For Deborah Madison's simple side dish, use thick, sturdy asparagus spears, which hold up better for high-heat roasting than the pencil-thin variety. Presoaking in cold water will keep the spears from shriveling in the oven.

1 Cut off tough ends of asparagus and discard. With a vegetable peeler, peel lower two-thirds of stalks. Soak in a bowl of cold water while oven preheats to 450°F (230°C). Drain asparagus and put in a gratin dish. Toss with oil and season with sea salt. Bake until stalks are tender when pierced with tip of a sharp knife, 15–25 minutes, depending on thickness.

2 Meanwhile, in a small skillet, heat citrus juice to achieve a simmer. Reduce juice to about 1½ table-spoons liquid. Remove from heat. Whisk in butter, a few chunks at a time, then add zest, rosemary, a pinch of sea salt, and pepper to taste.

3 When asparagus is done, remove from oven and transfer to a platter. Drizzle with sauce and serve.

Pickled Carrots with Fennel and Lemon

1 lb (500 g) baby carrots or slender young carrots

½ teaspoon fennel seeds

zest from 1 lemon, peeled in strips

1 cup (8 fl oz/250 ml) white wine vinegar

2 tablespoons sugar

1½ teaspoons pickling salt

MAKES 1 QT (1 L)

Quick pickles are perfect for those who can't wait weeks or months for their produce to be preserved; these are ready to eat in a matter of days. The jars make colorful table decorations and travel well—they're particularly wonderful for picnics.

1 In a large pot of boiling water, blanch carrots for 1 minute. Immediately transfer to a large bowl filled with ice water to halt cooking. Drain well.

2 Place carrots, fennel seeds, and lemon zest strips in a sterilized 1-qt (1-l) jar.

3 In a nonaluminum saucepan, bring remaining ingredients and 1 cup (8 fl oz/250 ml) water to a boil, stirring to dissolve sugar and salt. Remove from heat and ladle liquid over carrots in jar. Let cool to room temperature and then seal jar.

4 Refrigerate for 2 days before serving.

Vinegar-Glazed Tomatoes

2–3 large meaty tomatoes,
ripe but firm

3 tablespoons unsalted butter

1 large shallot, finely diced

1 tablespoon aged red wine vinegar

2 tablespoons balsamic vinegar

sea salt and freshly ground
black pepper

4 fresh opal basil leaves, torn
or shredded

4 large pieces country-style bread,
grilled or toasted and rubbed
with garlic

SERVES 4

For this recipe, use red summer tomatoes, such as Brandywine or Marmande. This dish is a delicious accompaniment to grilled chicken or flank steak.

1 Core tomatoes and cut into wedges about 1¼ inches across at widest point.

2 In a skillet large enough to hold tomatoes in a single layer, melt butter over medium-high heat. When it foams, add shallot and tomatoes and sauté, turning until color of tomatoes begins to dull, about 3 minutes.

3 Add vinegars and shake pan back and forth until they have reduced and a dark, thick sauce forms, about 5 minutes. Remove from heat. Season to taste with salt and plenty of pepper. Stir in basil leaves. Spoon alongside or atop garlic-rubbed toasts.

7

Just about everyone loves dessert, but agreement usually ends there. Some people crave layer cakes, others favor ice cream, and still others choose pies, tarts, or cookies. But the fiercest debates often come down to flavorings. While certain dessert lovers will argue that the best sweet endings are made with fresh fruits, others contend that no meal is complete without a chocolate finish. The best solution for a party? Serve a large selection of desserts to satisfy as many opinionated palates as possible.

desserts

Although it's the last course of the meal, a delicious dessert can make even the most wonderful dinner party doubly memorable. San Francisco pastry chef Emily Luchetti wins kudos from her guests with a trio of her favorite cakes: a decadent triple-layer chocolate cake with chocolate frosting, a creamy cappuccino-spiked cheesecake with a chocolate cookie crust, and her version of the creamsicle, vanilla ice cream and raspberry sorbet sandwiched between layers of sponge cake. For purists who want ice cream and nothing more, scoop up Apricot and Almond Praline Ice Cream, with its caramel-almond crunch swirled through a delicate fruit base, or the unusual—and unusually delectable—Sweet Pea Ice Cream, garnished with fried mint leaves. Also out of the ordinary is the quartet of silky, sweet

TORRONE BIANCO CON
ARANCIA CANDITA
ING.: ZUCCHERO, MANDORLA, MIELE,
ALBUME, GLUCOSIO, VANILLINA,
ACQUA, SURR. DI CIOCC. CONS. E 200
ARANCIA CANDITA

jellies included here. When sweet but simple bitefuls are the finale, serve confections made of fruits and nuts such as pecan brittle enlivened by a sprinkling of black pepper, sugar-dusted cocoa-almond rounds, and jewel-like candied citrus peels.

Because the dessert arrives at the end of the meal, it must complement everything that has gone before it. If you have served a showy starter and a rich main course, a light and uncomplicated dessert—a plate of crunchy biscotti, a refreshing sorbet—is in order. But if the starter and main course have been relatively simple, the dessert can be more lavish, such as an apple tart sweetened with chestnut purée or a multilayered strawberry shortcake. And if any small, easily portable confections remain uneaten at the end of the evening, pack them up for your guests to carry home as instant, edible party favors.

Marbled Chocolate Meringues

3 oz (90 g) bittersweet chocolate, chopped

4 egg whites

1 cup (8 oz/250 g) sugar

MAKES 20 COOKIES

Drizzling melted chocolate into the beaten egg whites, a clever trick from Robyn Valarik, creates strikingly marbled meringues. Even with chocolate, the cookies are feather light.

1 Preheat oven to 275°F (135°C). Line 2 baking sheets with parchment (baking) paper.

2 In a saucepan, bring 1–2 inches (2.5–5 cm) water to a simmer. Put chocolate in a heatproof bowl over (but not touching) simmering water and melt, stirring occasionally. Set aside and let cool slightly.

3 In another heatproof bowl, combine egg whites and sugar over (but not touching) simmering water and whisk until mixture is hot, 4–5 minutes. Remove bowl from heat. Using an electric mixer, beat on high speed until stiff peaks form and mixture is lukewarm, 4–5 minutes.

4 Drizzle melted chocolate over egg white mixture, folding in with a rubber spatula until just marbled.

5 With a soup spoon, drop batter in large mounds spaced 1½–2 inches (4–5 cm) apart on prepared sheets. Bake until crisp outside and still chewy inside, 35–40 minutes. Transfer sheets to a wire rack and let cool completely before removing cookies from parchment. Store in an airtight container.

Raspberry Creamsicle Cake

1⅓ cups (7 oz/220 g) all-purpose (plain) flour

½ teaspoon baking powder

¼ teaspoon salt

5 tablespoons (2½ oz/75 g) unsalted butter, softened

¾ cup (6 oz/185 g) sugar

2 eggs

grated zest of 1 orange

½ cup (4 fl oz/125 ml) fresh orange juice

3 pints (48 fl oz/1.5 l) good-quality vanilla ice cream

2 pints (32 fl oz/1 l) good-quality raspberry sorbet

raspberries for garnish (optional)

SERVES 12–16

Knowing that sometimes there can't be too much of a good thing, Emily Luchetti adds a bracing layer of raspberry sorbet to her ice cream cake. It's a wonderful dessert for an adult party as well as a child's.

1 Preheat oven to 350°F (180°C). Spray a 9-inch (23-cm) square baking pan with nonstick cooking spray and line bottom with parchment (baking) paper.

2 In a bowl, sift together flour, baking powder, and salt. Set aside.

3 In bowl of a standing mixer fitted with paddle attachment, cream butter and sugar until light and fluffy. Add eggs one at a time, beating well after each addition. Add orange zest. Add orange juice and flour mixture to batter alternately in 2 separate additions. Mix until blended. Spread in prepared pan.

4 Bake until a wooden skewer inserted into center comes out clean, 20–25 minutes. Remove from oven and let cool in pan for 10 minutes. Run a knife along inside edge of pan and invert onto a cake rack. Carefully peel off parchment and let cool completely. Use a serrated knife to cut cake in half horizontally. Carefully remove top layer and set aside. Return bottom layer to baking pan.

5 Let ice cream and sorbet stand at room temperature for 10 minutes. In bowl of a standing mixer fitted with paddle attachment, beat vanilla ice cream until smooth. Spread half of ice cream on top of cake layer in pan. Put remaining vanilla ice cream in freezer. Beat raspberry sorbet in same manner; when smooth, spread over ice cream in pan. Remove remaining ice cream from freezer and spread over sorbet. Place top cake layer on ice cream and press down lightly. Cover with plastic wrap and freeze until hard, at least 2 hours or preferably overnight.

6 Fill sink with about 2 inches (5 cm) hot tap water. Remove cake from freezer and dip pan in sink for a few seconds. Invert cake onto a cutting board; trim sides with a hot, dry knife. Cut into bars, and garnish with raspberries, if you like.

Cocoa-Almond Morsels

1½ cups (7 oz/220 g) slivered
blanched almonds

1 cup (4 oz/125 g) confectioners'
(icing) sugar

½ cup (1½ oz/40 g) cocoa powder

½ teaspoon almond extract (essence)

1 tablespoon rum

MAKES ABOUT 30 MORSELS

If you prefer, make Deborah Madison's confections
with a slightly crunchy exterior: Reduce the
cocoa powder to ¼ cup (¾ oz/20 g), adding it all
to the almonds, and roll the balls in superfine
(caster) sugar.

1 In a food processor, process almonds with confectioners'
sugar until extremely fine, 1–2 minutes. Add ¼ cup (¾ oz/
20 g) cocoa powder and almond extract. Mix thoroughly.
While pulsing motor, add rum and 2–3 teaspoons water
to form a stiff dough.

2 Place remaining cocoa powder on aluminum foil. Pinch
off dough and roll to form 1-inch (2.5-cm) balls. Roll
each ball in cocoa powder; place in a fluted paper cup.

Apple and Yogurt Torta

2 cups (10 oz/315 g) all-purpose
(plain) flour

1 teaspoon baking powder

¼ teaspoon salt

3 eggs

½ cup (4 oz/125 g) whole-milk
plain yogurt

2 tablespoons plus 1½ teaspoons
Colonna Bergamia oil or other
citrus-infused olive oil

1½ cups (12 oz/375 g)
granulated sugar

2 apples, peeled, cored, and sliced
into thin wedges

1 teaspoon confectioners' (icing)
sugar, for dusting

SERVES 8

This delicious cake is a sweet specialty at Marina Colonna's olive oil ranch on the southeastern coast of Italy. Use real citrus-infused oil rather an artificially flavored one.

1 Preheat oven to 350°F (180°C). Lightly grease a 9-inch (23-cm) springform pan. Line base with buttered parchment (baking) paper.

2 In a large bowl, sift together flour, baking powder, and salt. In a separate bowl, beat eggs, yogurt, and oil until smooth. In alternating additions, gradually beat granulated sugar and flour mixture into egg mixture until a thick batter forms. Fold in half of apples.

3 Pour mixture into prepared cake pan and smooth surface. Arrange remaining apples on top. Bake until golden and a wooden skewer inserted into center comes out clean, about 1¼ hours. Remove from oven and let cool in pan for 10 minutes. Run a knife around inside edge of pan and remove pan sides. Invert cake and remove base of pan. Carefully peel off parchment. Transfer to wire rack right side up and let cool completely. Dust top with confectioners' sugar.

Blackberry Jelly

4 cups (1 lb/500 g) blackberries, plus more for garnish

½ cup (4 oz/125 g) sugar

1 envelope plain gelatin

juice of ½ lemon

almond oil for oiling molds

fresh mint leaves, for garnish

SERVES 6

Flavorless almond oil works well for oiling gelatin molds. To turn the jelly out onto a serving plate, Alison Attenborough suggests running the tip of a knife around the rim of the mold and then dipping the mold briefly in hot water to loosen.

1 In a bowl, combine 4 cups (1 lb/500 g) berries and sugar. Let stand for 2 hours. Push through a fine-mesh sieve with back of a large spoon. Discard seeds.

2 In another bowl, sprinkle gelatin over ½ cup (4 fl oz/125 ml) cold water. Let stand until softened, about 5 minutes. Add ½ cup (4 fl oz/125 ml) boiling water and stir to dissolve. Stir in blackberry purée and lemon juice. Lightly oil 6 individual ¾-cup (6–fl oz/185-ml) molds or ramekins. Divide mixture among molds. Refrigerate until set, at least 6 hours.

3 Unmold onto serving plates and garnish with berries and mint.

Candied Citrus Peels

2 red grapefruits or 6–8 oranges

1½ cups (12 oz/375 g) granulated sugar

¼ cup (2 fl oz/60 ml) light corn syrup

1 cup (8 oz/250 g) superfine (caster) sugar, plus more for storage

FOR DIPPING (OPTIONAL)

4 oz (125 g) semisweet (plain) or bittersweet chocolate

1 tablespoon unsalted butter

MAKES ABOUT 1 LB (500 G) CANDIED PEELS

Candied zest contrasts bright citrus flavors with a shield of sugar. They're a divine end to the perfect dinner party. If you make mixed peels, Deborah Madison recommends cooking the different types separately so you can remove each from the heat when it's done.

1 Scrub fruit to remove any waxy coating. Score fruits into quarters and peel (reserve flesh for another use). Put peels in a saucepan, cover with cold water, and bring to a boil for 1 minute. Drain peels; cover again with cold water. Place a heavy plate on top to keep peels submerged. Bring to a boil, lower heat to low, and simmer for 30 minutes. Remove pan from heat; let stand until liquid reaches room temperature, or as long as overnight. If pith is very thick, scrape away excess. Slice peel into strips.

2 Combine granulated sugar, corn syrup, and 1½ cups (12 fl oz/ 375 ml) water in a 3-qt (3-l) saucepan and bring to a boil over high heat. When sugar is dissolved and syrup is clear, add peels. Lower heat to low and cook slowly until translucent, about 1 hour. Transfer peels to a wire rack set over a tray to catch drips.

3 Pour superfine sugar onto a plate. When peels are cool enough to handle, roll each peel in sugar to coat, then return it to drying rack for 1 hour. Coat a second time with sugar, then return to rack to dry for 1 hour longer. If not dipping in chocolate, sprinkle bottom of an airtight container with superfine sugar. Arrange peels in a tight layer and sprinkle with more sugar. Arrange remaining peels in layers, sprinkling with sugar between each layer. Cover and refrigerate.

4 If dipping in chocolate, melt chocolate with butter in top of a double boiler set over simmering water. Stir to blend thoroughly.

5 Dip ends of cooled peel into melted chocolate, coating just 1 end. Transfer to a sheet of wax paper and set in a cool place to harden. Store in sugar as described above.

Chestnuts in Syrup

1½ cups (12 oz/375 g) sugar

1 whole vanilla bean

½ lb (250 g) peeled whole chestnuts,
fresh or vacuum-packed

MAKES ½ LB (250 G) CHESTNUTS

Glistening and translucent amber, Fran Gage's preserved chestnuts make delectable holiday gifts packed into pretty glass jars. Serve over chocolate ice cream, as shown, or use them to make Chestnut Roulade (page 274).

1 In a heavy saucepan, combine sugar and 1 cup (8 fl oz/250 ml) water. Split vanilla bean in half lengthwise. Using a small, sharp knife, scrape seeds into pan, then add pod. Cook over medium heat, stirring occasionally, until sugar is dissolved. Bring to a boil.

2 Add chestnuts. (If using vacuum-packed nuts, separate carefully so they don't break apart.) Bring syrup to a simmer. Simmer until chestnuts look translucent but are still firm, about 25 minutes for packaged nuts and a little longer for fresh ones. Remove from heat and let cool.

3 Transfer to a jar and store in refrigerator. The chestnuts will keep in their syrup for several weeks.

Cactus Pear Sorbet

½ cup (4 oz/125 g) sugar

2 strips lemon zest

3 fresh mint sprigs

8 cactus pears (about 3 lb/1.5 kg total weight)

SERVES 4

Cactus pears, also known as prickly pears, grow on cactus trees, as the name suggests. Depending on the variety of cactus, the fruit varies in color from yellow to pink to brilliant orange.

1 In a small saucepan, combine sugar, 1 cup (8 fl oz/250 ml) water, lemon zest, and mint over medium-low heat, stirring occasionally, until sugar is dissolved. Bring to a boil and cook until a light syrup forms, about 5 minutes. Pour into a bowl, set aside, and let cool completely. Discard lemon zest and mint sprigs.

2 Meanwhile, halve cactus pears and scoop out flesh; put skins in a bowl, cover with plastic wrap, and refrigerate. In a food processor, purée cactus pear flesh, add cooled syrup, and process to blend. Press through a fine-mesh sieve and discard seeds. Transfer mixture to a bowl, cover with plastic wrap, and refrigerate for 1 hour.

3 Freeze cactus pear mixture in an ice-cream maker according to manufacturer's instructions. Transfer to a freezer-proof container and freeze until serving.

4 Select the best reserved cactus pear skins, allowing 1 skin per serving. Arrange in small bowls and fill each skin with a scoop of sorbet.

Chocolate Layer Cake

1½ cups (4½ oz/140 g) cocoa powder

3 cups (15 oz/470 g) all-purpose (plain) flour

1¼ teaspoons baking powder

1¼ teaspoons baking soda (bicarbonate of soda)

½ cup (4 oz/125 g) plus 2 tablespoons unsalted butter, softened

2¼ cups (1 lb/ 500 g) firmly packed light brown sugar

3 eggs

1¼ cups (10 fl oz/310 ml) buttermilk

FROSTING

4 oz (125 g) bittersweet chocolate, chopped

8 oz (250 g) unsweetened chocolate, chopped

1 cup (8 oz/250 g) unsalted butter

3 cups (12 oz/375 g) confectioners' (icing) sugar

⅛ teaspoon salt

¾ cup (6 fl oz/180 ml) milk

SERVES 8–10

Most classic American cakes aren't show-off affairs, but one kind does demand a pedestal and that's a layer cake, particularly if it's all chocolate. Including both buttermilk and boiling water in the batter ensures that the layers are moist.

1 Preheat oven to 350°F (180°C). Spray bottoms of three 9-inch (23-cm) cake pans with nonstick spray. Place a parchment (baking) paper circle inside each pan.

2 In a small saucepan, bring 1¼ cups (10 fl oz/310 ml) water almost to a boil. Put cocoa powder in a bowl and whisk in hot water to make a smooth paste. Let cool slightly. In another bowl, sift together flour, baking powder, and baking soda. Set aside.

3 In bowl of a standing mixer fitted with paddle attachment, beat butter and brown sugar on medium-high speed until smooth and light. Add eggs one at a time, beating well after each addition. On low speed, add half of flour mixture to butter mixture and then half of buttermilk. Repeat with remaining flour mixture and buttermilk. Stir in cooled cocoa paste.

4 Divide batter evenly among 3 pans. Bake until a wooden skewer inserted into center comes out clean, 20–25 minutes. Remove from oven and let cool in pans for 10 minutes. Run a knife around inside edge of each pan and invert onto wire racks. Peel off parchment and let cool completely.

5 FOR FROSTING: Melt chocolates and butter in top pan of a double boiler over low heat. Whisk to combine. Remove from heat and let cool to room temperature.

6 Sift confectioners' sugar into a large bowl. Whisk in salt and milk. Add chocolate mixture and whisk until smooth. Frost top of each cake layer, placing 1 layer on top of another. Spread frosting around sides of cake.

Dates Stuffed with Rose-Almond Paste

20 large dates, such as Medjool
or Black Sphinx

7 oz (220 g) almond paste

1 teaspoon rose water

1–2 drops red food coloring

20 candied organic rose petals
for garnish

MAKES 20 STUFFED DATES

Middle Eastern flavors are married in Deborah Madison's elegant stuffed dates. To enhance the effect, sprinkle with chopped pistachio nuts.

1 Slit dates open lengthwise and remove pits.

2 In a food processor, pulse almond paste with rose water and food coloring, adding coloring one drop at a time until paste is a delicate shade of pink.

3 Transfer almond paste to a work surface and roll into a 10-inch (25-cm) log. Cut into 20 equal pieces. Roll each piece into an oval shape and insert into a date. Slice dates in half so that ingredients are visible. To serve, place each stuffed date on a candied rose petal.

Prunes with Candied Citrus Peels and Chocolate

20 moist pitted prunes

20 small Candied Citrus Peels
(page 257)

20 small chunks bittersweet
chocolate

superfine (caster) sugar

MAKES 20 STUFFED PRUNES

Deborah Madison's prunes are an incredibly easy and luscious after-dinner recipe. If you don't have time to make your own candied peels, purchase them at a specialty-foods store. For a formal occasion, place each stuffed prune in an individual fluted paper cup.

1 With your fingers, enlarge opening of each pitted prune. Insert a piece of candied orange zest and a chunk of chocolate. Close prune. Roll in superfine sugar and place in a fluted paper cup.

Apple Tart with
Chestnut Purée

The browned custard peeking out around the apples is the first hint that this is not an ordinary apple tart. It can take guests a surprisingly long time to guess that chestnuts are the secret ingredient.

TART DOUGH

½ cup (4 oz/125 g) plus 2 tablespoons unsalted butter, softened

¾ cup (3 oz/90 g) confectioners' (icing) sugar

pinch of salt

½ teaspoon cognac

1 egg, at room temperature, lightly beaten

1¾ cups (9 oz/280 g) unbleached all-purpose (plain) flour

3 apples

1 can (17½ oz/545 g) sweetened chestnut purée or *crème de marron*

2 eggs

⅓ cup (3½ oz/105 g) apricot preserves

SERVES 8

1 FOR TART DOUGH: In bowl of a standing mixer fitted with paddle attachment, beat butter. Add confectioners' sugar, salt, and cognac and mix well. With motor running, gradually add beaten egg. Beat until well blended, scraping down sides of bowl once or twice. Turn off mixer, add flour, and then mix on low speed until just combined. Dough will be soft and sticky. Wrap in plastic wrap and flatten to a disk 1 inch (2.5 cm) thick. Refrigerate until firm, at least 1 hour.

2 Place a rack in center of oven and preheat to 375°F (190°C). Unwrap dough. If dough is very cold, beat with a rolling pin to make more malleable. On a lightly floured work surface, roll out dough into a 13-inch (33-cm) round about ⅛ inch (3 mm) thick. Carefully fit dough into a 9-inch (23-cm) fluted tart pan with removable bottom. Trim excess dough from around edges. Freeze tart shell for 20 minutes.

3 Line tart shell with parchment (baking) paper or aluminum foil and fill with pie weights or dried beans. Bake until sides are set, about 10 minutes. Remove weights and parchment or foil. Continue baking until bottom is set, 5 minutes longer.

4 Peel apples and cut in half vertically. Remove cores with a melon baller or sharp knife. Lay apple halves flat and cut into slices 1/16 inch (2 mm) thick, keeping slices together. Discard very short end pieces.

5 In a bowl, whisk sweetened chestnut purée and eggs to combine. Pour mixture into tart shell. Arrange apple slices in overlapping, concentric circles to cover chestnut filling completely. Bake until chestnut purée is set and apples are browned, about 40 minutes.

6 Let cool in pan. Remove pan sides and base. In a small saucepan, combine apricot preserves with 2 tablespoons water. Warm over low heat until preserves melt, then strain through a fine-mesh strainer. Brush on top of tart.

Strawberry Ice Cream Sandwiches

¾ cup (6 fl oz/180 ml) milk

3 egg yolks

½ cup (4 oz/125 g) sugar

1 lb (500 g) strawberries, hulled

¾ cup (6 fl oz/180 ml) heavy (double) cream

CHOCOLATE DISKS

8 oz (250 g) bittersweet or semisweet (plain) chocolate, chopped

SERVES 10

Wafers made from melted bittersweet or semisweet chocolate are a crisp and delectable enclosure for summery strawberry ice cream. A balance of milk and heavy cream results in a satisfyingly dense texture.

1 In a small saucepan, warm milk over medium heat just until bubbles appear around edge of pan. Remove from heat and set aside. Meanwhile, in a bowl, beat egg yolks with sugar. Stir in warm milk. Wipe pan clean and pour in custard mixture. Cook over medium-low heat, stirring constantly, until just thick enough to coat back of a spoon, 5–8 minutes. Immediately remove from heat and strain through a fine-mesh sieve into a clean bowl. Place plastic wrap directly on custard surface. Let cool to room temperature, then refrigerate for at least 1 hour.

2 In a blender or food processor, purée strawberries, in batches if necessary. Strain through a fine-mesh sieve. Transfer to a bowl, cover, and refrigerate for 1 hour.

3 In a large bowl, whisk together cold custard and strawberry purée. In a separate bowl, beat cream until soft peaks form. Fold into custard mixture. Freeze in an ice-cream maker according to manufacturer's instructions. Transfer to a freezer-proof container and freeze.

4 FOR CHOCOLATE DISKS: Put chopped chocolate in a heat-proof bowl, set over a pan of simmering water, and melt, stirring occasionally, until smooth, about 10 minutes. Remove from heat.

5 On a smooth sheet of aluminum foil, spread chocolate in a layer ¹⁄₁₆ inch (2 mm) thick. Let cool completely. When set, cut out disks using a 2½-inch (6-cm) round cookie cutter.

6 Remove ice cream from freezer 10 minutes before serving. Sandwich each scoop of ice cream between 2 chocolate disks.

Chestnut Roulade

4 eggs, at room temperature

⅓ cup (3 oz/90 g) plus 1 tablespoon granulated sugar

¼ cup (1 oz/30 g) cake (soft-wheat) flour, sifted

CHESTNUT WHIPPED CREAM

1 cup (8 fl oz/250 ml) heavy (double) cream

½ cup (5 oz/155 g) sweetened chestnut purée

confectioners' (icing) sugar, for dusting

Chestnuts in Syrup (page 258) or *marrons glacés*, for garnish

SERVES 12–14

1 Place a rack in center of oven. Preheat oven to 475°F (245°C). Line an 18-by-12½-inch (45-by-32-cm) rimmed baking sheet with parchment (baking) paper and butter sides. Separate 2 eggs, setting whites aside. In bowl of a standing mixer fitted with whisk attachment, combine 2 egg yolks and 2 whole eggs. Beat at medium speed, gradually adding ⅓ cup (3 oz/90 g) granulated sugar. Increase speed to high and beat until egg mixture is thick, pale, and almost doubled in volume. Transfer to another bowl.

2 Wash and dry bowl and whisk. In bowl, beat egg whites with whisk until foamy. Add 1 tablespoon sugar. Increase speed to high and beat until soft peaks form. Fold whites into egg mixture.

3 Sift flour over egg mixture (this is a second sifting) and fold in. Pour batter onto prepared baking sheet and spread as evenly as possible over sheet. Bake on center rack for 3 minutes. Rotate sheet so cake bakes evenly and continue to bake until cake is golden, 4 minutes longer. Remove from oven. Run a table knife around edges and slide out cake, still on parchment. Let cake cool, paper side down, on wire rack. When cool, lift paper and cake and return to cooled baking sheet. Cover with plastic wrap and refrigerate until needed.

4 FOR CHESTNUT WHIPPED CREAM: In a bowl, whip cream until soft peaks form. In a small bowl, mix sweetened chestnut purée with a small amount of whipped cream, then fold mixture into remaining cream.

5 Place cake, paper side up, on another piece of parchment. Carefully peel off top piece of paper. Trim edges of cake to facilitate rolling. Spread whipped cream on cake with an icing spatula.

6 With a long side of the cake toward you, roll into a log. Transfer to a serving plate, placing seam side down. With a sharp knife, cut a diagonal piece from each end of log to form a clean edge. Dust with confectioners' sugar. Wipe plate clean with a paper towel. Garnish cake with chestnuts in syrup or *marrons glacés*. Refrigerate until serving.

Strawberry Cream Cake

1¼ cups (6½ oz/200 g) all-purpose (plain) flour

2½ teaspoons baking powder

⅛ teaspoon salt

5 eggs, separated

1¼ cups (10 oz/315 g) granulated sugar

1½ teaspoons vanilla extract (essence)

grated zest of 2 lemons

STRAWBERRY CREAM FILLING

2 cups (½ lb/250 g) fresh strawberries, hulled and thinly sliced, plus more for garnish

1 teaspoon fresh lemon juice

4–6 tablespoons (2–3 oz/60–90 g) granulated sugar

2 cups (16 oz/500 g) crème fraîche

⅔ cup (5 fl oz/160 ml) heavy (double) cream

1 teaspoon vanilla extract (essence)

confectioners' (icing) sugar, for dusting

SERVES 8–10

This impressive dessert is an oversized version of strawberry shortcake. Add a minimal amount of sugar to the berries and taste them for sweetness before adding more.

1 Preheat oven to 350°F (180°C). Line base of a 9-inch (23-cm) springform pan with parchment (baking) paper. In a bowl, sift together flour, baking powder, and salt. Set aside.

2 In bowl of a standing mixer fitted with whisk attachment, whisk together egg yolks and sugar on high speed until thick; mixture will still be grainy. Reduce to medium-low speed and add 5 tablespoons (2½ fl oz/75 ml) boiling water. Turn off mixer and scrape down sides and bottom of bowl. On high speed, whisk again until thick. Stir in vanilla and lemon zest. On low speed, stir in flour mixture.

3 In a separate bowl, beat egg whites on medium-low speed until frothy. Increase to medium-high speed and beat until thick and smooth but not dry. Fold half of whites into batter. Then fold in remaining whites.

4 Gently spread batter in prepared pan. Bake until a wooden skewer inserted into center comes out clean, 35–40 minutes. Let cool in pan for 10 minutes. Run a knife around inside edge of pan and remove pan sides. Invert cake and remove base of pan. Carefully peel off parchment. Transfer to a wire rack and let cool completely. Use a serrated knife to cut cake horizontally into 3 layers.

5 FOR FILLING: Place strawberries in a bowl; stir in lemon juice and 2 tablespoons granulated sugar. Taste for sweetness; depending on berries' ripeness, you may need to add 1–2 more tablespoons sugar. In bowl of a standing mixer fitted with whisk attachment, combine crème fraîche, cream, vanilla, and 2 tablespoons granulated sugar on medium-high speed. Beat until soft peaks form and cream holds its shape.

6 Place 1 cake layer on serving plate. Arrange one-third of strawberries and juices over cake. Spread one-third of cream over berries. Repeat layering process with remaining 2 cake layers, ending with a layer of cream.

7 Just before serving, dust top of cake with confectioners' sugar. Cut with a serrated knife.

Hungarian Pancakes with Walnuts and Chocolate

1 cup (8 fl oz/250 ml) milk

3 eggs

1¼ cups (6½ oz/200 g) all-purpose (plain) flour

1 teaspoon sugar

pinch of salt

1 cup (8 fl oz/250 ml) club soda

¼ cup (2 oz/60 g) unsalted butter, melted

WALNUT FILLING

½ cup (4 fl oz/125 ml) half-and-half (half cream), plus more if needed

½ cup (4 oz/125 g) sugar

¼ cup (1½ oz/45 g) chopped golden raisins

1 teaspoon grated orange zest

2 cups (8 oz/250 g) finely chopped walnuts

2 tablespoons light rum

CHOCOLATE SAUCE

4 oz (125 g) semisweet (plain) chocolate, chopped

¾ cup (6 fl oz/180 ml) milk

3 egg yolks

2 tablespoons *each* sugar, unsweetened cocoa powder, and light rum

1 tablespoon unsalted butter

¼ cup (2 oz/60 g) butter, plus more if needed

SERVES 8

1 In a blender, combine milk, eggs, flour, sugar, and salt and blend at medium-high speed until very smooth, about 1 minute. Transfer to a bowl, cover, and let rest for about 30 minutes. Just before cooking, stir club soda into batter.

2 Heat an 8-inch (20-cm) crêpe pan over medium-high heat. Lightly coat bottom of pan with butter. Holding pan away from heat and at an angle, pour a scant ¼ cup (2 fl oz/60 ml) batter into pan and quickly tip and tilt pan until bottom is thinly and evenly coated. Return to heat and cook until golden on bottom, about 1 minute. Turn pancake over and cook for about 10 seconds longer. Transfer to a plate first side down. Repeat process, stacking pancakes, until all batter is used (makes about 16 pancakes). Cover with plastic wrap.

3 FOR FILLING: In a saucepan, combine half-and-half and sugar and bring just to a simmer over medium heat, stirring gently. Stir in raisins, orange zest, walnuts, and rum. Simmer for 1 minute. Set aside and keep warm.

4 FOR SAUCE: In a small saucepan over very low heat, melt chocolate. Watch carefully and stir occasionally to be sure chocolate does not scorch. Set aside. In another saucepan, heat milk gently over medium heat. Do not allow to boil.

5 Meanwhile, in a small bowl, whisk egg yolks with sugar and cocoa powder until smooth. Gradually whisk in hot milk. Return to saucepan and cook over very low heat, stirring, until mixture coats back of a spoon, 4–6 minutes. Do not allow to boil. Remove from heat and stir in melted chocolate, rum, and 1 tablespoon butter. Keep warm.

6 To assemble, spread about 2 tablespoons filling onto each pancake. (If filling is too thick, stir in a little half-and-half.) Fold each pancake into quarters. Melt butter in a large skillet and add filled pancakes, a few at a time. Turn pancakes to coat with butter, and cook until heated through, adding more butter if needed. Arrange 2 pancakes on each warmed dessert plate, drizzle with warm chocolate sauce, and serve.

Red Currant and Raspberry Jelly

2 envelopes plain gelatin

1 cup (8 oz/250 g) sugar

1 cup (4 oz/125 g) fresh raspberries

1 cup (4 oz/125 g) fresh red currants, plus currants for garnish

½ cup (4 fl oz/125 ml) black currant vodka

SERVES 4

Alternating layers of red currant-raspberry jelly and black currant vodka-spiked jelly make Alison Attenborough's dessert a study in stripes and berry flavors.

1 In a small bowl, sprinkle gelatin over ¼ cup (2 fl oz/ 60 ml) water. Let stand until softened, about 5 minutes. In another bowl, combine sugar with 1¾ cups (14 fl oz/430 ml) boiling water. Stir to dissolve. Add to gelatin mixture and stir to dissolve gelatin. Divide between 2 large glass measuring pitchers.

2 In a blender, purée raspberries and red currants. Strain through a fine-mesh sieve. Add berry purée to 1 measuring pitcher of gelatin mixture and stir to blend. Add vodka to other measuring pitcher of gelatin mixture and stir to blend.

3 Divide half of berry mixture among 4 individual 1-cup (8–fl oz/250-ml) gelatin molds. Refrigerate until set, about 1 hour. Divide half of vodka mixture among molds. Refrigerate until set, about 45 minutes. Repeat with remaining portions of berry and vodka mixtures, refrigerating until set after each addition, to produce 4 layers per mold. To serve, unmold onto individual serving plates.

Moroccan Mint Tea Jelly

2 envelopes plain gelatin

1 tablespoon green tea leaves

¼ cup (1¾ oz/55 g) superfine (caster) sugar

2 cups (2½ oz/75 g) packed fresh mint leaves, plus mint sprigs for garnish

SERVES 4

Serve cubes of this Moroccan flavored jelly, a different take on iced tea, in tall glasses for a light and elegant ending to a meal. Like mint tea, it can be cooling in the summer and restorative in winter.

1 In a bowl, sprinkle gelatin over 1 cup (8 fl oz/250 ml) water. Let stand until softened, 5 minutes.

2 Put tea leaves in a teapot and add 3 cups (24 fl oz/750 ml) boiling water. Let steep for 5 minutes. Strain tea and discard leaves. Stir in superfine sugar to dissolve. Add mint leaves and let steep for 5 minutes to infuse. Strain through a fine-mesh sieve into gelatin mixture.

3 Rinse an 8-inch (20-cm) square baking dish and pour gelatin mixture into wet dish. Refrigerate until set, about 4 hours. Cut gelatin into cubes. Spoon into iced tea glasses or glass bowls and garnish with mint sprigs.

Orange and Campari Jelly

2½ cups (20 fl oz/625 ml) fresh orange juice

2 envelopes plain gelatin

½ cup (4 oz/125 g) sugar

½ cup (4 fl oz/125 ml) Campari

juice of 1 lemon

orange slices, for garnish

SERVES 6

Jellies can—and indeed must—be made in advance. They look as beautiful when cut up and spooned into glasses or compote dishes as they do when unmolded onto dessert plates.

1 Strain orange juice through a fine-mesh sieve and discard any pulp. In a bowl, sprinkle gelatin over 1 cup (8 fl oz/250 ml) orange juice. Let stand until softened, about 5 minutes. In a small saucepan, combine sugar with 1 cup (8 fl oz/250 ml) water. Over medium heat, bring to a boil, stirring to dissolve sugar. Pour over gelatin mixture and stir to dissolve.

2 Add remaining orange juice, Campari, and lemon juice. Divide among 6 Campari glasses or wineglasses. Refrigerate until set, at least 6 hours. To serve, garnish with orange slices.

Citrus Angel Food Cakes

10 egg whites, at room temperature

1¼ teaspoons cream of tartar

1½ cups (12 oz/375 g) granulated sugar

1 cup (3 oz/90 g) cake (soft-wheat) flour, sifted

⅛ teaspoon salt

grated zest of 1 orange

grated zest of 1 lemon

grated zest of 1 lime

GLAZE

¼ cup (2 fl oz/60 ml) fresh lime juice

1¼ cups (5 oz/155 g) confectioners' (icing) sugar

finely grated lemon zest, for garnish

MAKES 8

A mix of citrus adds sweet piquancy to airy individual angel food cakes, which are decorated with a simple glaze. Alternatively, bake the batter in a 10-inch (25-cm) angel food pan for about 40 minutes to make one large cake. Serve with fresh berries, if you like.

1 Preheat oven to 350°F (180°C). Have ready 8 ungreased 4-inch (10-cm) angel food cake pans.

2 In bowl of a standing mixer fitted with whisk attachment, beat egg whites on medium-low speed until frothy, about 30 seconds. Add cream of tartar. Increase to medium-high speed and beat for 15 seconds longer. With machine running, add granulated sugar in a slow, steady stream. Beat until whites are thick and satiny; they should be stiff but still moist.

3 Reduce to low speed and carefully beat in flour, salt, and citrus zests. Gently spread batter into angel food cake pans. Tap pans on counter to eliminate any air bubbles.

4 Bake until a wooden skewer inserted into center comes out clean, about 20 minutes. Remove from oven and let cool completely in pans upside down. Run a knife around inside edge of each pan and tube and gently remove cakes. Place on wire racks.

5 FOR GLAZE: In a small bowl, combine lime juice and confectioners' sugar. Stir until smooth and free of lumps. Drizzle glaze over each cake and sprinkle with lemon zest.

Pecan Brittle
with Black Pepper

1 cup (4 oz/125 g) pecans

1 cup (8 oz/250 g) sugar

½ cup (5 oz/155 g) corn syrup

½ teaspoon salt

½–1 teaspoon freshly ground
black pepper

1½ tablespoons unsalted butter,
cut in pieces

MAKES ABOUT ¾ LB (375 G)

It's unconventional, but a generous grinding of black pepper accentuates the sweetness and nuttiness of Deborah Madison's pecan brittle. A candy thermometer is indispensable for this recipe, to ensure that the brittle has the correct bite.

1 Preheat oven to 350°F (180°C). Spread pecans on a baking sheet and toast until fragrant and starting to darken, 5–7 minutes. Lightly butter a rimmed baking sheet. Spread pecans in a single, close layer in pan.

2 In a 2-qt (2-l) saucepan, combine sugar and corn syrup with ½ cup (4 fl oz/125 ml) water. Cook over medium heat, swirling pan until sugar is completely dissolved. Cover pan and cook for 1 minute longer. Uncover and continue to cook without stirring, until syrup is a medium amber color and registers 295°F (145°C) on a candy thermometer (hard-ball stage).

3 Remove caramel from heat and stir in salt and pepper, then butter. Mixture will foam up. Pour over nuts while still foamy, spreading it out a little. When cool, break into pieces. Store in an airtight container.

Sweet Pea Ice Cream

3 cups (15 oz/470 g) shelled fresh peas (about 3 lb/1.5 kg in the shell)

1 cup (8 fl oz/250 ml) milk

⅓ cup (3 oz/90 g) sugar

2 fresh mint sprigs

1 cup (8 fl oz/250 ml) heavy (double) cream

finely grated zest and juice of 1 lemon

SERVES 4–6

The flavoring of this ice cream—peas, usually reserved for savory dishes—isn't the only thing that's unusual about Barbara Kafka's dessert. Mint leaves, fried quickly in a flavorless vegetable oil, make a daring optional garnish.

1 Combine peas, milk, sugar, and mint sprigs in a 2-qt (2-l) saucepan and bring to a simmer over medium heat. Cover, lower heat to low, and cook, stirring occasionally, until peas are mushy, about 25 minutes. Cooking liquid will mostly be absorbed by peas.

2 In a blender, combine pea mixture and cream. Purée until very smooth. Strain through a fine-mesh sieve and stir in lemon zest and juice. Transfer mixture to a stainless-steel bowl. Cover and refrigerate for 2 hours or until well chilled.

3 Freeze mixture in ice-cream maker according to manufacturer's instructions. Transfer to an airtight container and freeze until serving.

Chocolate Brioches

1 package (¼ oz/7 g) active
dry yeast

3 tablespoons lukewarm milk
(100°–110°F/38°–43°C)

4 cups (1¼ lb/625 g) all-purpose
(plain) flour, plus more if needed

⅓ cup (1 oz/30 g) cocoa powder

½ cup (4 oz/125 g) sugar

1 teaspoon salt

7 eggs, at room temperature,
lightly beaten

1 cup (8 oz/250 g) unsalted
butter, softened

4 oz (125 g) bittersweet chocolate,
chopped in ¼-inch (6-mm) pieces

vegetable oil for coating

1 egg beaten with 1 tablespoon
water, for egg wash

MAKES FOURTEEN 2½-INCH
(6-CM) BRIOCHES

Perfect on their own, Robyn Valarik's brioches also serve well as the base for elegant desserts. Slice them and top with ice cream and chocolate shavings, or butter the slices and toast them, then layer with raspberries and whipped cream.

1 In a liquid measuring pitcher, combine yeast and milk. Stir until dissolved. Let stand until foamy, 5–10 minutes.

2 In bowl of a standing mixer fitted with dough hook, combine flour, cocoa powder, sugar, and salt. Add yeast mixture and eggs. Beat on medium-low speed until ingredients are blended and dough is smooth, about 5 minutes. With machine running, add butter, 1–2 tablespoons at a time, blending well after each addition. Continue mixing until dough is shiny and elastic and begins to pull away from sides of bowl, 4–5 minutes. If dough does not pull away from sides, mix in additional flour 2 tablespoons at a time. Do not add too much; dough should be sticky. Mix in chopped chocolate.

3 Coat a large bowl lightly with vegetable oil. Transfer dough to bowl and cover with plastic wrap. Let rise until nearly doubled in volume, about 2 hours. Transfer dough to a lightly floured surface. Punch down and shape into a ball. Return dough to oiled bowl, cover with plastic wrap, and let rise in refrigerator overnight.

4 Remove dough from refrigerator, punch down, and transfer to a lightly floured work surface. Divide dough in half, then divide each half into 7 equal-sized pieces. Roll each piece into a ball and place smooth side up in paper brioche or panettone molds. Place filled molds on a baking sheet and cover loosely with plastic wrap. Let rise again at room temperature until almost doubled in size, 1½–2 hours.

5 Meanwhile, preheat oven to 350°F (180°C). Lightly brush dough with egg wash. Bake until brioches have a hollow sound when tapped, about 35 minutes. Transfer to a wire rack and let cool.

Caramelized Walnuts Stuffed with Almond Paste

40 fresh walnut halves

3½ oz (105 g) almond paste

½ cup (4 oz/125 g) sugar

2 tablespoons light corn syrup

MAKES 20 STUFFED WALNUTS

If it's humid, the caramel may soften or become sticky, so wait to coat the nuts until just before serving in this sophisticated recipe by Deborah Madison. If you like, let the caramel thicken slightly, then dip a fork in it and wave it over the stuffed walnuts to enclose them in a nest of caramel threads.

1 Preheat oven to 350°F (180°C). Spread walnuts on a baking sheet and toast until fragrant but not dark, 5–6 minutes. Remove and let cool.

2 Roll almond paste into a 10-inch (25-cm) log and slice into 20 equal pieces. Roll each piece into a ball. Press between 2 walnut halves to form a spherical shape. Place on a wire rack set over a sheet of aluminum foil.

3 In a small saucepan, combine sugar, corn syrup, and 2 tablespoons water, swirling pan to dissolve sugar. Place over medium-high heat and cook until syrup turns a light golden color. Watching carefully, cook until syrup is amber or until a candy thermometer registers 265°F (130°C). Immediately remove from heat. Do not overcook; syrup will continue to darken when removed from heat.

4 While syrup is cooling and still thin, pick up nuts with a pair of chopsticks or tongs and dip them into syrup; return to rack. Let cool, turning once to prevent sticking.

Cornmeal Cupcakes with Pecan Frosting

1 cup (5 oz/155 g) all-purpose (plain)
flour

1¼ teaspoons baking powder

⅓ cup (2 oz/60 g) yellow cornmeal

¼ teaspoon salt

½ cup (4 oz/125 g) plus 1 tablespoon
unsalted butter, softened

1¼ cups (10 oz/315 g)
granulated sugar

3 eggs

½ cup (4 oz/125 g) sour cream

FROSTING

6 oz (185 g) cream cheese, softened

⅓ cup (3 oz/90 g) unsalted butter,
softened

¼ cup (1 oz/30 g) confectioners'
(icing) sugar

½ teaspoon vanilla extract (essence)

3–4 tablespoons heavy (double) cream

¼ cup (1 oz/60 g) toasted, chopped
pecans, plus 3 pecan halves, thinly
sliced

MAKES 6 CUPCAKES

Both the buttery cornmeal cakes and cream cheese frosting can be made ahead, but don't frost the cupcakes until the day you serve them. Let the unfrosted cupcakes stand overnight at room temperature, wrapped well, or freeze them. Cover and refrigerate the frosting.

1 Preheat oven to 350°F (180°C). Spray 6 muffin pan cups (¾-cup/6–fl oz/180-ml capacity) with non-stick cooking spray. In a bowl, sift together flour and baking powder. Stir in cornmeal and salt. Set aside.

2 In bowl of a standing mixer fitted with paddle attachment, cream butter and sugar until light and fluffy. Add eggs one at a time, beating well after each addition. In 3 separate additions, add flour mixture and sour cream alternately, blending well after each addition.

3 Divide batter among muffin pan cups. Bake until a wooden skewer inserted into center comes out clean, 25–30 minutes. Remove from oven; when cool to touch, unmold and let cool completely on wire racks before frosting.

4 FOR FROSTING: In bowl of a standing mixer fitted with paddle attachment, beat cream cheese until smooth. Add butter and sugar and beat until smooth. Stir in vanilla, cream, and chopped pecans.

5 Frost cupcakes. Sprinkle sliced pecans on top of each. Refrigerate. Let stand at room temperature for 30 minutes before serving.

Chocolate Mousse Cake

CHOCOLATE SPONGE CAKE

⅔ cup (3 oz/90 g) sifted all-purpose
(plain) flour

⅓ cup (1 oz/30 g) cocoa powder

¼ teaspoon salt

6 large eggs, at room temperature

1 tablespoon vanilla extract (essence)

1 cup (8 oz/250 g) sugar

CHOCOLATE MOUSSE

6 oz (185 g) bittersweet chocolate,
chopped

3 tablespoons unsalted butter

2 tablespoons dark rum

1 teaspoon vanilla extract (essence)

1½ teaspoons unflavored gelatin

3 large eggs, at room temperature,
separated

3 tablespoons plus ¼ cup
(2 oz/60 g) sugar

¼ teaspoon cream of tartar

½ cup (4 fl oz/125 ml) heavy (double)
cream, chilled

chocolate curls, for garnish

SERVES 8–10

1 FOR SPONGE CAKE: Preheat oven to 350°F (180°C). Line an 18-by-13-inch (45-by-33-cm) rimmed baking sheet with parchment (baking) paper and set aside.

2 In a bowl, sift together flour, cocoa powder, and salt; set aside. In another bowl, combine eggs and vanilla. Using an electric mixer, beat on high speed until light and pale yellow, about 10 minutes. Slowly add sugar and continue to beat for 2–3 minutes. Sift one-fourth of flour mixture over egg mixture and fold in. Repeat 3 more times with remaining flour mixture. Pour batter into prepared pan and spread evenly. Bake until a wooden skewer inserted into center comes out clean, 25–30 minutes. Let pan cool completely on a wire rack.

3 FOR MOUSSE: In top of a double-boiler, combine chocolate, butter, rum, and vanilla and stir until melted and blended. Transfer to a small bowl and set aside. Meanwhile, in another small bowl, sprinkle gelatin over 3 tablespoons water and let stand for 5 minutes to soften.

4 In clean double boiler, combine egg yolks, gelatin mixture, and 3 tablespoons sugar and whisk constantly until thick and pale yellow, 6–7 minutes. Remove from heat and whisk into melted chocolate mixture. Set aside and let cool.

5 In a bowl, beat egg whites with an electric mixer on medium-high speed until soft peaks form. Beat in cream of tartar. Gradually add remaining ¼ cup (2 oz/60 g) sugar. Increase to high speed and continue beating until peaks are stiff. Stir one-third of beaten egg whites into cooled chocolate mixture. Fold in remaining whites. In a clean bowl, beat cream on medium-high speed until soft peaks form. Fold cream into chocolate mixture.

6 To assemble, turn cooled cake out onto cutting board, peel off parchment, and cut into 4 equal-sized rectangles. Turn 1 rectangle upside down and place on serving plate. Spread with one quarter of the mousse and top with another rectangle of cake. Repeat, alternating layers, ending with mousse. Refrigerate for at least 4 hours or up to overnight. Trim cake sides to reveal layers. Garnish with chocolate curls.

Three Melon Sorbets

2 lb (1 kg) melon cubes
(see headnote)

½ cup (4 oz/125 g) sugar

juice from 1 lime

SERVES 8–12

Make this sorbet three times, each with a different variety and color of melon, such as watermelon, honeydew, and cantaloupe.
The amount of lime juice added to the sorbet depends on the ripeness of each melon.
Add a little at a time, tasting between additions.

1 Discard any seeds from melon cubes. In a food processor, process melon until smooth. Add sugar and half of lime juice and process again. Taste, adding more lime juice if needed. Strain through a fine-mesh sieve into a clean bowl.

2 Refrigerate melon purée until very cold, about 1 hour. Freeze in an ice-cream maker according to manufacturer's instructions. Transfer to a freezer-proof container and freeze until serving. Repeat process with other types of melon.

Cappuccino Cheesecake

CRUST

1 cup (8 oz/250 g) cold unsalted
butter, cut into small pieces

½ cup (4 oz/125 g) granulated sugar

1¼ cups (6½ oz/200 g) all-purpose
(plain) flour

¼ cup (1½ oz/45 g) rice flour

½ cup (1½ oz/45 g) cocoa powder

large pinch of salt

FILLING

1½ lb (750 g) cream cheese, softened

1 cup (8 oz/250 g) granulated sugar

4 eggs

2 cups (16 oz/500 g) sour cream

2 tablespoons instant espresso
powder, preferably Medaglia d'Oro

GLAZE

½ cup (3½ oz/105 g) firmly packed
dark brown sugar

½ cup (4 oz/125 g) unsalted butter

¼ cup (2 fl oz/60 ml) heavy
(double) cream

cocoa powder, for dusting

SERVES 8–10

The base for Emily Luchetti's decadent cheesecake is like a brownie. To save a step and make a crisper crust, you can crush chocolate wafers and add enough melted butter so the crumbs hold together, then press into the pan and bake as directed.

1 FOR CRUST: In bowl of a standing mixer fitted with paddle attachment, combine all crust ingredients. Mix on low speed until dough comes together. Roll dough into a 9-inch (23-cm) circle. Pat into base of a 9-inch (23-cm) springform pan. Refrigerate for at least 30 minutes or up to overnight.

2 Preheat oven to 300°F (150°C). Bake crust for 30 minutes. Let cool completely.

3 FOR FILLING: In bowl of a standing mixer fitted with paddle attachment, beat cream cheese on medium speed until smooth. Add granulated sugar and again beat until smooth. Add eggs one at a time, beating well after each addition. Stir in sour cream and espresso powder. Mix until smooth.

4 Pour filling into crust and spread evenly. Place pan in a large roasting or baking pan; then place on oven rack. Carefully fill roasting pan halfway up sides of springform pan with hot water. Bake until cake looks set from center to edges, but not dry, when pan is gently shaken, about 1¼–1½ hours.

5 Remove from oven and let cool at room temperature for 30 minutes. Refrigerate until chilled throughout, about 1 hour.

6 FOR GLAZE: In a small, heavy saucepan, combine brown sugar, butter, and cream over low heat until sugar is dissolved. Raise heat to high and bring to a boil. Reduce heat to medium and cook, stirring constantly, until thick and smooth. Let cool to room temperature.

7 When ready to serve, remove cheesecake from refrigerator and transfer to a large serving plate. Cut with a hot, dry knife. Serve slices drizzled with caramel glaze and dusted with cocoa powder.

Lemon Verbena Ice Cream with Poached Asian Pears

2 cups (16 fl oz/500 ml) milk

1 cup (1 oz/30 g) tightly packed fresh
lemon verbena leaves

1 cup (8 oz/250 g) sugar

4 egg yolks, lightly beaten

1½ cups (12 fl oz/375 ml) heavy
(double) cream

POACHED ASIAN PEARS

½ cup (4 oz/125 g) sugar

2 cups (16 fl oz/500 ml) Sauternes

½ vanilla bean, split horizontally

2 firm but ripe Asian pears, peeled
and quartered

SERVES 8–10

1 In a small saucepan over medium heat, combine milk and lemon verbena leaves. Bring to just below boiling point. Remove from heat, cover, and let stand for 30 minutes.

2 In a bowl, combine sugar and egg yolks. Stir in lemon verbena–infused milk mixture, including leaves. Wipe pan clean and return mixture to pan. Cook over medium-low heat, stirring constantly, until thick enough to coat back of a spoon, about 10 minutes. Remove from heat and strain through a fine-mesh sieve into a clean bowl, discarding lemon verbena leaves. Cover with plastic wrap pressed directly on surface of custard to prevent a skin from forming. Let cool completely, then refrigerate for 1 hour.

3 In a bowl, beat cream until soft peaks form. Fold whipped cream into chilled custard. Freeze mixture in an ice-cream maker according to manufacturer's instructions. Transfer to a freezer-proof container and freeze until ready to serve.

4 FOR POACHED ASIAN PEARS: In a small saucepan, combine sugar, wine, and vanilla bean over low heat until sugar is dissolved. Boil for 5 minutes. Add pears and pour in enough water to completely cover fruit. Cover with a piece of parchment (baking) paper and then lid. Poach for 1 hour. Remove from heat and let fruit cool in syrup. Transfer fruit to a bowl, discarding vanilla bean. Boil syrup rapidly over high heat until reduced to 1 cup (8 fl oz/250 ml). Pour syrup over fruit. Cover and refrigerate until ready to serve.

5 Serve scoops of ice cream topped with poached pears and drizzled with syrup.

Chocolate Pistachio Biscotti

1½ cups (7½ oz/235 g) all-purpose (plain) flour

⅓ cup (1 oz/30 g) cocoa powder

1½ teaspoons baking powder

pinch of salt

½ cup (4 oz/125 g) unsalted butter, softened

½ cup (4 oz/125 g) granulated sugar

¼ cup (2 oz/60 g) firmly packed light brown sugar

2 eggs

1½ teaspoons vanilla extract (essence)

1 cup (4 oz/125 g) shelled unsalted pistachios

6 oz (185 g) semisweet (plain) chocolate, coarsely chopped (about 1 cup)

MAKES 2 DOZEN COOKIES

Robyn Valarik makes her biscotti with two kinds of chocolate—cocoa powder in the dough, punctuated by chunks of semisweet chocolate—to intensify the impact. These biscotti will keep for weeks; serve for tea or an after-dinner sweet. Store them in an airtight plastic bag in the freezer.

1 Preheat oven to 350°F (180°C). Line a baking sheet with parchment (baking) paper. In a bowl, sift together flour, cocoa powder, baking powder, and salt. Set aside.

2 In a large bowl, combine butter, granulated sugar, and brown sugar with a wooden spoon. Add eggs one at a time, beating well after each addition. Stir in vanilla. Add half of flour mixture and stir until blended; repeat with remaining flour mixture. Stir in pistachios and chocolate.

3 Transfer dough to a lightly floured work surface and shape into a log about 16 inches (40 cm) long, 2½ inches (6 cm) wide, and 1½ inches (4 cm) high. Put log on parchment-lined baking sheet and flatten log slightly. Bake until surface is firm and slightly cracked, about 25 minutes. Let cool completely on a wire rack.

4 Lower oven temperature to 300°F (150°C). Transfer cooled log to cutting board. Using a serrated knife, cut into slices ⅓ inch (9 mm) thick. Put slices cut side down on same parchment-lined baking sheet and bake until crisp, 15–20 minutes. Transfer to a wire rack to cool.

glossary

Amaranth A green with a slightly sweet flavor that can be used both in cooking and for salads. Amaranth, also called Chinese spinach, is available in two colors, green and red (or burgundy). The small, very young baby leaves, usually sold in small bundles, are delicate in appearance and flavor. Look for amaranth in specialty-food stores and Asian produce markets.

Artichokes, baby Like all artichokes, baby artichokes are edible members of the thistle family. Most so-called baby artichokes are fully mature, but are grown lower down on the plant than their larger counterparts, where the lack of sun keeps them small. They lack a choke (the fuzzy material inside), and the whole vegetable can be used once the tough, fibrous green outer leaves are trimmed away. Look for fresh baby artichokes in specialty-food stores and produce markets; if you cannot find them, you may substitute standard globe artichokes, trimmed and cut into quarters, in most preparations.

Arugula This peppery, tender green, very popular in Italy, is also known as *rocket, roquette, rucola,* or *rugula.* Arugula is becoming more readily available in supermarkets and produce markets. If you cannot find it, substitute any favorite green; mildly bitter greens such as escarole work well.

Asian pears Also called apple pears, these firm, round fruits are golden in color. Their flavor is like that of pears, though slightly less sweet, but their flesh is very crisp and juicy, like that of apples. Look for them at farmers' markets and produce markets from late summer through fall. Store them in the refrigerator.

Caper/caperberry Small, round capers are the buds of a Mediterranean bush that have been pickled or preserved with salt. Caperberries, most often imported from Spain, are a salty, preserved form of the mature fruit of the bush. They are about the size of a small olive.

Champagne vinegar Vinegar made from champagne has a delicate flavor that is well suited to dressing salads with equally delicate ingredients. It can be found in specialty-food stores. If it is unavailable, substitute a good-quality white wine vinegar.

Chanterelle mushroom See *Mushrooms.*

Chestnuts A starchy nut, grown both in Europe and America, that can be used in sweet or savory dishes. Chestnuts have a hard, glossy, dark- brown shell that must be removed before use; to do so, cut an X in the shell with a sharp knife and roast the chestnuts in a 400ºF oven until the shells pull away from the meat. When just cool enough to handle, pull off both the outer shell and the inner peel of each nut. Whole cooked, peeled chestnuts can be purchased vacuum-packed; those preserved in jars with liquid tend to fall apart when used in recipes.

Chestnut purée, sweetened Sweetened chestnut purée (sometimes called sweetened chestnut spread) is available in specialty-food stores and from baking-supply companies. This smooth paste saves labor when making chestnut-based desserts. When choosing chestnut purée for baking, make sure it is adequately sweetened; heavy unsweetened or lightly sweetened chestnut purée is sometimes available but is not suitable for baking. High-quality crème de marron, imported from France, is a sweet, light purée made from chestnuts preserved in sugar.

Chickpeas Also known as garbanzo bean or ceci, this nutty-tasting, tan, round member of the pea family is sold both dried and canned. The dried form requires long soaking and cooking; a good-quality canned product is an acceptable substitute in many cases.

Chiles Native to the Americas, hot chiles have been adapted by cuisines throughout the world. Chiles may be dried or fresh, and many varieties are available in supermarkets. Chiles used in this book include the following types.

AJÍ AMARILLO CHILE These yellow, piquant chiles are one of the distinctive flavors of Peruvian cuisine. Hot ají amarillo purée is a bright orange-yellow color; it comes packed in jars and is used in sauces or to garnish dishes. Whole chiles, packed in brine, are also available; they may be chopped for use in ceviches. Jars of mixed Peruvian chiles also usually contain ají amarillo. Look for both forms of ají amarillo at Latino markets, particularly those specializing in South American imports. If they are unavailable, substitute any favorite hot chile, roasted, peeled, and seeded (and processed to a paste for ají amarillo purée).

HUNGARIAN CHERRY CHILE Also called cherry pepper, this chile is round and bright red; its small size (1 to 2 inches in diameter) emphasizes its resemblance to the cherry. Its heat can range from mild to medium, but it also has a slightly sweet flavor. It is available at specialty-food stores fresh, pickled in jars, and dried.

Citrus oil There are two types of citrus oil: pure citrus oils made by cold-pressing natural oils from the zest of citrus fruits, and flavored oils made by blending or infusing neutral oils with citrus fruit flavors. Pure citrus oils are quite expensive and intensely flavored; use them in baking or in small quantities. For salads or other dishes in which you want a subtle citrus flavor, use infused or blended citrus oils. Look in specialty-food shops for high-quality or naturally pressed citrus oils.

Couscous A wheat product similar to pasta, but with much lighter, smaller grains. Couscous is commonly eaten in North Africa as a base for stews; some types, such as Israeli couscous, have larger, round grains. Couscous can be prepared very quickly by steaming or cooking in water; it is now widely available in supermarkets and specialty-food stores.

Crème fraîche A French-style, lightly soured and thickened fresh cream, generally used as a topping or garnish for savory or sweet dishes. Crème fraîche is available in supermarkets and specialty-food stores. To make crème fraîche yourself, stir 1 teaspoon cultured buttermilk into 1 cup (8 fl oz/250 ml) heavy (double) cream. Cover tightly and leave at warm room temperature until thickened, about 12 hours. Refrigerate until ready to serve. Crème fraîche will keep for up to 1 week in the refrigerator.

Currants A small berry related to the gooseberry, currants are grown worldwide but may be more widely available in Europe and Britain than in the United States. The fresh fruit is not to be confused with dried currants, which are not actually currants at all, but the dried form of the tiny zanté grape. Fresh currants have a tart-sweet flavor; the flavor of black currants tends to be less bright than the red. Both black and red currants are used in jams and jellies; black currants are the base for the French liqueur crème de cassis. Look for fresh currants in specialty-produce markets; they are most commonly available from June through August.

Dandelion greens The green, saw-toothed young leaves of dandelions have a tangy, slightly bitter flavor. Tiny baby leaves are delicate and delicious; use them on their own or mix with more mature leaves. Dandelion greens are available in many produce markets and farmers' markets.

Dates A desert fruit that grows in clusters on date palms. Dates are extremely sweet and come in three types: soft (which are plump and very moist), semi-dry (favored in the United States for their low moisture, firm texture, and good flavor), and dry or bread dates (which are hard and dry with a high sugar content). The recipes in this book use the following types of dates.

MEDJOOL Often considered the king of dates, the Medjool is a very large soft date that is reddish-brown in color when ripe and not quite as moist as many soft dates. Along with semi-dry varieties, Medjools are preferred in the United States.

BLACK SPHINX Developed in Arizona and not widely grown, Black Sphinx dates are smaller than Medjools and have an excellent deep, rich flavor. They are available in some specialty-food stores.

Dulce de leche Literally "milk sweetness," this Mexican caramel is made by slowly cooking milk and sugar until the sugar is caramelized and the milk has turned thick and golden brown. It can be made at home or purchased in Latin markets and some supermarkets. *Cajeta,* a similar caramel made from goat's milk, can be substituted; if using *dulce de leche* over ice cream or as a sauce for other desserts, any favorite caramel sauce may be substituted.

Endive Belgian endive, also called chicory or witloof, is a member of the family of chicories—leafy vegetables with a distinctive bitter flavor. The smooth white (sometimes red), candle-shaped heads, or *chicons,* of endive leaves have a mild flavor. At the market, look for endive that is properly stored away from light; the best will be tightly furled and white, with no brown blemishes or hints of green on the outer leaves.

Espresso powder Instant espresso powder is a powdered form of coffee that is often used in recipes where coffee flavor is desirable but additional liquid is not. It provides more intense flavor than instant coffee, but instant coffee may be substituted if espresso powder is unavailable. If you can find only instant espresso granules (not powder), crush them with a rolling pin or process briefly in a blender or food processor to produce a quick-dissolving powder.

Fava beans A bean used in Mediterranean cooking, fava beans (also called broad beans) are bright green when fresh. They grow in thick pods; these must be removed before use, as must the tough skin that surrounds all but the very youngest fava beans. Look for the fresh beans at produce markets, especially in Italian neighborhoods. Frozen fava beans are sometimes available at specialty-produce markets. If they are unavailable, substitute fresh or frozen lima beans. Some people of Mediterranean descent may have a hereditary condition called *favism* that causes an adverse reaction to fava beans, so use caution if eating favas for the first time.

Fennel, baby Fennel is a crisp, mildly anise-flavored bulb vegetable, also referred to by its Italian name, finòocchio. Small young bulbs are sometimes sold as baby fennel and have a delicious, subtle flavorare sometimes sold as baby fennel; they have a delicious, subtle flavor. If they are unavailable, substitute mature fennel and use some of the fronds to approximate the baby variety's delicate flavor.

Fingerling potatoes These small potatoes, named for their shape, are irregularly long and thin. Some new varieties have golden flesh or reddish skins. Fingerlings are usually harvested young and are delicious roasted or steamed. If you cannot find fingerling potatoes at farmers' markets or produce markets,

and a flavor slightly reminiscent of cantaloupe. Pepino melons can be found in specialty-produce markets.

Pistou A French version of the more familiar Italian pesto, pistou is a sauce or condiment made by pureeing or grinding together basil, garlic, and olive oil. It lacks the pine nuts and cheese that are commonly added to pesto. The word *pistou* can also apply to a French vegetable soup that is topped with a basil-garlic sauce.

Plantains Plantains, often used in Latin American and African cooking, are a member of the banana family. When green, they are firm, starchy, and bland; as they ripen, the skin blackens and they become softer and slightly sweeter. Plantains can be roasted, baked, fried, or mashed. Look for them in Latin markets or specialty-produce markets.

Pomegranates These fall and winter fruit have a leathery red skin enclosing inner membranes full of edible seeds, each covered with juicy, translucent ruby-red pulp. To use the seeds, carefully pull the pomegranate apart with your fingers and pull each seed away from the membrane. Pomegranates can be juiced much like citrus fruits, using an electric juicer.

Porcini mushroom See *Mushrooms.*

Pine nuts Called *pignoli* in Italian, pine nuts are small, ivory-colored seeds that come from the cones of certain species of pine cones. They are labor-intensive to harvest and thus can be expensive, but they are widely available in specialty-food shops and many supermarkets. They have a unique, slightly resinous flavor and are used often in Italian cooking.

Prosciutto The sine qua non of Italian hams, prosciutto is salt-cured and aged a minimum of 10 months, which produces a dense, richly flavored meat that is ofen served thinly sliced as an appetizer with fruits such as figs or melons.

Red chile powder Chile powder, made of ground dried red chiles, is distinct from the generic spice mix sold as chili powder in supermarkets (usually a blend of chiles, cumin, oregano, and other spices). Red chile powder ranges from mild (as with ancho chile powder) to incendiary (as with cayenne or powder made from chiles pequín), depending on the chile used. Chile powders are becoming more widely available in supermarkets, but if your market does not carry them, look for specific types of chile powder in Latin markets or substitute paprika and cayenne, blended to the heat level you desire. Do not substitute chili powder.

Rice Cultivated for thousands of years, rice is a staple grain for many cultures around the world. Long-, medium-, and short-grained varieties are readily available in specialty-foods stores. Rice varieties used in this book include the following.

ARBORIO RICE A popular Italian variety with short, round grains high in starch content, which creates a creamy, sauce-like consistency during cooking. It is most often used for risotto and is available in Italian delicatessens and some supermarkets.

CARNAROLI RICE An Italian rice of the *superfino* grade, Carnaroli is ideal for making stiff risottos that form the base for strong flavors. It has large, tapered, glassy grains with a thick coating of starch, which rubs off during the cooking process to create risotto's characteristic creaminess. If Carnaroli rice is unavailable, substitute Arborio.

VIALONE NANO RICE A fino variety of Italian rice used for risotto. Because it has smaller grains than superfino-grade rice varieties such as Arborio, it produces a less stiff, more fluid risotto, known in Italy as *all'onda*. Look for Vialone Nano rice in specialty-food shops and Italian groceries; if it is unavailable, another Italian rice, such as Arborio or Carnaroli, may be substituted for risotto, but the texture of the finished dish will be thicker.

Rice flour A finely ground flour made from white rice, rice flour is commonly used in Asian cooking (especially that of Southeast Asia) to make noodles and crêpes. Rice flour is also used in baking, though because it lacks gluten it may not be substituted directly for wheat flour in most recipes. Look for rice flour in Asian markets and specialty-food stores, as well as some supermarkets.

Rose water An extremely aromatic, sweetly perfumed flavoring liquid, distilled from rose petals. Rose water is used in desserts, especially those of India and the Middle East. It is available in specialty-food stores and baking-supply stores.

Saffron Made of the dried stigmas of a crocus and very labor-intensive to produce, saffron is one of the most expensive foods in the world. A small pinch of it, however, is usually sufficient to add its characteristic aromatic flavor and bright gold color to a dish. It comes in two forms: threads, which should be measured very loosely packed, and powdered. Saffron is usually soaked in a small amount of liquid before it is added to any dish.

Samphire There are two plants commonly called samphire: rock samphire (native to the coasts of Britain and Europe and now rare) and *salicorne* or *salicornia*. Found on both coasts of North America and also called marsh samphire, sea bean, or sea pickle, the latter is the type more commonly found in the

United States. Both types have spiky leaves and are crisp, aromatic, and salty. Samphire is mainly sold pickled in jars; it can be found in some specialty-food stores.

Savory An herb related to the mint family. The two types of savory, summer and winter savory, are similar, though the latter is stronger in flavor. Either may be used in most recipes calling for savory. The herb is available dried, but as with most herbs is better fresh. Savory complements chicken, fish and bean dishes.

Spinach, magenta A bright purple-red variety of spinach, also sometimes called ruby spinach. When picked extremely young (as a small seedling), it is a microgreen. Use the tender, flavorful microgreens in salads or as a garnish. Some specialty-produce markets or farmers' markets carry microgreens; if they are unavailable, substitute baby spinach leaves.

Squash There are two basic types of squash, winter and summer. Winter squash generally have dense orange or golden flesh and resemble gourds and are large and heavy. Smaller summer squash, such as zucchini, lack the tough skin and do not require long cooking. Their flesh is tender, and they are best used when small and freshly picked. Types of squash used in this book include the following.

ACORN SQUASH A dark green, ridged oval squash with very tough skin. It is often cut in half and baked after the seeds are scooped out, as its ridges make it difficult to peel. To cut it in half, use a large, sharp knife or cleaver.

BUTTERNUT SQUASH A pale yellowish tan winter squash with yellow to orange flesh. About 8–12 inches (20–30 cm) long, it has a broad bulblike base and a slender neck. It is widely available and can be substituted for other winter squashes.

ZUCCHINI SQUASH/BLOSSOMS This familiar summer squash, also known as courgette, comes in several different varieties: the ubiquitous dark green, a golden yellow, and a slightly rounder pale green type. Whatever the color, zucchini is best when it is young and tender. Choose zucchini that are firm to the touch. The pale yellow-orange flowers of zucchini and other summer squash are fully edible, but they must be used when very fresh. They have a delicate squash flavor and are often stuffed and fried or shredded and eaten raw in salads or other cold dishes.

Tamari sauce A Japanese-style sauce made from fermented soybeans. Similar to but mellower in flavor than soy sauce, tamari can be found in Asian markets and many supermarkets. If it is unavailable, substitute soy sauce, preferably low-sodium.

Tamarind A sour fruit used in Indian, Southeast Asian and Middle Eastern cooking, the tamarind grows in pods that contain seeds and a dark pulp that is concentrated to a thick consistency. Tamarind pulp offers a distinctive sweet-sour edge to dishes. It is available as pulp, canned paste, whole pods or bricks in some Asian markets. If unavailable, substitute fresh lime juice mixed with a small amount of molasses.

Tatsoi An Asian green with a flavor similar to bok choy. It is most often available in Asian markets and specialty-food stores as loose baby leaves, which are round and dark-green with white stems; it often is one of the greens in a mixture sold for stir-frying. If tatsoi is unavailable, bok choy may be substituted in many preparations.

Treviso radicchio A variety of radicchio that differs from the more familiar round variety (*radicchio di Verona*) in the shape of its head, which is elongated and less tightly compacted, with long, spear-shaped tapering leaves. Treviso radicchio leaves are a bright magenta color, with white ribs at the center; they are bitter and can be used raw or cooked. Treviso radicchio can be found in produce markets or specialty-food stores; if it is unavailable, substitute common radicchio or Belgian endive.

Truffle/truffle oil The truffle is a much-sought-after and very expensive fungus with a unique earthy flavor and aroma. One small truffle will perfume a large dish. Truffles may be black or white (slightly milder). Look for them in late fall to midwinter in specialty-food shops. Truffle oil is oil (usually a mildly-flavored olive oil) that has been infused with the flavor of truffles. Truffles are often shaved over a dish at the last minute to retain their fresh flavor; similarly, truffle oil will dissipate if added to a dish too early, so it is best to drizzle it over the finished dish just before serving.

Yellow wax beans These pale-yellow fresh beans are similar in flavor and texture to common green beans. They can be found in produce markets and some supermarkets year-round; the best quality will be available from May through October. If they are unavailable, any type of green beans may be substituted.

Zest The fragrant outermost skin layer of citrus fruit (usually oranges or lemons), which can be removed with a paring knife, vegetable peeler, or a citrus zester. Only the colored portion of the skin (and not the white pith) is considered zest.

Zucchini squash/blossoms See *Squash.*

index

acknowledgments

Weldon Owen would like to thank the talented TASTE magazine editorial team, particularly editor-in-chief Andy Harris and creative director Emma Ross. A special thanks to Teri Bell, Tanya Henry, John Jaxheimer, Kate Krader, Jackie Mallorca, Richard Van Oosterhout, Stephanie Owen, Maggie Ruggiero, Sharon Silva, and Kate Washington. We would also like to thank the following photographers for their fine work: Sang An, Burcu Avsar, Quentin Bacon, Ben Dearnley, Miki Duisterhof, Lisa Hubbard, John Kernick, David Loftus, Charles Maraia, William Meppem, Minh + Wass, Amy Neunsinger, Charles O'Rear, David Prince, Laurie Smith, Roger Stowell, Luca Trovato, and Anna Williams. We are grateful for the many wonderful recipes offered by the following writers: Alison Attenborough, Mario Batali, Arrigo Cipriani, Marion Cunningham, Sara Deseran, Craig Von Foerester, Fran Gage, Andy Harris, Barbara Kafka, Jeffery Lindenmuth, Emily Luchetti, Deborah Madison, Donata Maggipinto, Matt Millea, the Ravida family, Maggie Ruggiero, Bill Samuels, Jr., Anna Soprano, Robert Stehling, Nettie Symonette, Susie Theodorou, Robyn Valarik, Bobo Vincenzi, Chuck Williams, and Victoria Wise.

credits

AUTHORS: **ALISON ATTENBOROUGH**: Pages 252, 282, 286; **MARIO BATALI**: Pages 155, 156, 159, 162, 165, 166; **CAPEZZANA WINE AND CULINARY CENTER**: Page 73; **ARRIGO CIPRIANI**: Page 101; **GIUSEPPE CIPRIANI**: Page 40; **MARION CUNNINGHAM**: Pages 141, 144, 145, 148, 151; **SARA DESERAN**: Page 69; **CRAIG VON FOERESTER**: Page 191; **FRAN GAGE**: Pages 92, 102, 196, 258, 266, 274; **ANDY HARRIS**: Pages 25, 31, 36, 44, 49, 56, 70, 70, 172, 176, 185, 199, 204, 207, 211, 215; **BARBARA KAFKA**: Pages 55, 85, 89, 95, 186, 203, 222, 227, 293; **JEFFERY LINDENMUTH**: Page 26; **EMILY LUCHETTI**: Pages 245, 262, 277, 289, 298, 305; **DEBORAH MADISON**: Pages 60, 86, 96, 193, 212, 221, 232, 236, 248, 257, 265, 290, 297; **DONATA MAGGIPINTO**: Pages 43, 77, 129, 130, 133, 134, 137; **MATT MILLEA**: Page 110; **THE RAVIDA FAMILY**: Pages 119, 120, 123, 124; **MAGGIE RUGGIERO**: Page 235; **BILL SAMUELS, JR.**: Page 39; **ANNA SOPRANO**: Page 251; **ROBERT STEHLING**: Page 195; **NETTIE SYMONETTE**: Pages 32, 43; **SUSIE THEODOROU**: Pages 59, 63, 66, 74, 105, 106, 109, 113, 179, 182, 200, 228, 231, 261, 269, 273, 281, 302, 306; **ROBYN VALARIK**: Pages 242, 294, 301, 309; **BOBO VINCENZI**: Page 208; **CHUCK WILLIAMS**: Page 278; **VICTORIA WISE**: Page 175

PHOTOGRAPHERS: **SANG AN**: Pages 249, 256, 264, 291, 296; **BURCU AVSAR**: Page 247 (bottom left); **QUENTIN BACON**: Pages 5 (top right), 16 (bottom right), 18, 19 (top), 19 (bottom left), 19 (bottom right), 23 (bottom left), 28 (bottom right), 53 (bottom right), 68, 90, 91 (bottom right), 114, 152, 154, 157, 158, 163, 164, 167, 218, 240 (bottom left); **BEN DEARNLEY**: Pages 7 (top right), 10, 11, 65, 160 (top, left and right), 161 (top right), 209, 219 (top right), 250, 255 (top right; bottom); **MIKI DUISTERHOF**: Pages 58, 62, 67, 230; **LISA HUBBARD**: Pages 104, 107, 108, 112; **JOHN KERNICK**: Pages 57 (left), 194; **DAVID LOFTUS**: Pages 6, 7 (top left), 16 (bottom left), 17, 22, 23 (top left), 28 (top, left and right), 29 (top left; bottom left), 41, 54, 93, 100, 103, 116, 118, 121, 122, 125, 171 (top, left and right), 180, 181, 197, 223, 224 (bottom right), 225 (top right), 253, 259, 260, 267, 268, 272, 275, 280, 283, 287, 303, 307; **CHARLES MARAIA**: Page 183; **WILLIAM MEPPEM**: Cover, Pages 1, 4, 5 (bottom left), 7 (bottom right), 8, 12, 16 (top, left and right), 20, 23 (top right), 24, 28 (bottom left), 29 (top right; bottom right), 30, 33, 34, 35, 37, 38, 42 (right), 45, 48, 50, 52, 53 (top left), 57 (right), 71, 72, 75, 79, 82, 91 (top; bottom left), 98, 99, 146, 161 (bottom left), 168, 170, 173, 177, 178, 184, 188, 192, 198, 201, 205, 206, 210, 213, 214, 216, 219 (top left), 224 (top, left and right; bottom left), 225 (top left; bottom), 238, 240 (bottom right), 241 (top; bottom left), 246, 247 (top, left and right), 254, 255 (top left), 270, 271, 279, 284; **MINH + WASS**: Pages 88 (right), 138, 140, 142, 149, 150, 187, 202, 219 (bottom left), 234, 243, 295, 300, 308; **AMY NEUNSINGER**: Pages 2, 42 (left), 76, 83 (top left), 111, 126, 128, 131, 132, 135, 136, 171 (bottom left), 190, 247 (bottom right); **CHARLES O'REAR**: Pages 14, 64, 160 (bottom), 161 (top left), 161 (bottom right); **DAVID PRINCE**: Pages 61, 83 (top right), 87, 97, 220, 237; **LAURIE SMITH**: Pages, 5 (top left), 80; **ROGER STOWELL**: Pages, 46 (top left), 46 (top right), 46 (bottom left), 46 (bottom right), 47, 53 (bottom left); **LUCA TROVATO**: Pages 27, 83 (bottom left), 84, 94, 226, 292; **ANNA WILLIAMS**: Pages 174, 244, 263, 276, 288, 299, 304

WILLIAMS-SONOMA INC.
Founder & Vice Chairman: Chuck Williams
Book Buyer: Cecilia Michaelis

WILLIAMS-SONOMA TASTE
Editor in Chief: Andy Harris
Executive Editor: Victoria Spencer
Creative Director: Emma Ross

WELDON OWEN INC.
Chief Executive Officer: John Owen
President: Terry Newell
Chief Operating Officer: Larry Partington
Vice President International Sales: Stuart Laurence
Sales Manager: Emily Jahn
Creative Director: Gaye Allen
Publisher: Hannah Rahill
Associate Publisher: Val Cipollone
Art Director: Catherine Jacobes
Senior Editor: Sarah Lemas
Design Assistant: Teri Gardiner
Consulting Editor: Maggie Ruggiero
Copy Editors: Desne Ahlers, Arin Hailey, Kate Washington
Digital Production: Joan Olson
Production: Teri Bell, Chris Hemesath
Indexer: Ken DellaPenta

Recipes and photographs originally published in the USA, 2001-2002, in Williams-Sonoma TASTE Magazine © 2001–2002 Weldon Owen Magazines Inc. and Williams-Sonoma Inc.

TASTE RECIPES FOR ENTERTAINING
Conceived and produced by Weldon Owen Inc.
814 Montgomery Street, San Francisco, CA 94133
In collaboration with Williams-Sonoma Inc.
3250 Van Ness Avenue, San Francisco, CA 94109

Printed in Singapore by Tien Wah

A WELDON OWEN PRODUCTION
Copyright © 2002 Weldon Owen Inc. and Williams-Sonoma Inc.
All rights reserved, including the right of reproduction in whole or in part, in any form.

First printed in 2002
10 9 8 7 6 5 4 3 2 1

Library of Congress Cataloging-in-Publication Data is available

ISBN 1-892374-74-9